MEMOIRS OF A
FEN TIGER

KU-470-204

MR & MRS J M BELL
83 ST JAMES AVENUE
UPTON BY CHESTER
CHESHIRE
CH2 1NN
0244 43989

MEMOIRS OF A
FEN TIGER

AUDREY JAMES

A DAVID & CHARLES COUNTRY BOOK

British Library Cataloguing in Publication Data

James, Ernie, 1906-
    Memoirs of a Fen tiger: the story of Ernie.
    James of Welney as told to Audrey James.
    (A David & Charles country book).
    1. Norfolk. Welney. James, Ernie, 1906-
    Biographies
    I. Title   II. James, Audrey
    942.6'13

    ISBN 0-7153-9251-4

© Audrey James 1984

All rights reserved. No part of this
publication may be reproduced, stored
in a retrieval system, or transmitted,
in any form or by any means, electronic,
mechanical, photocopying, recording or
otherwise, without the prior permission
of David & Charles Publishers plc

First published in 1986 in hardback by David & Charles
Publishers plc. This paperback edition published
1988 by David & Charles Publishers plc
and printed in Great Britain by
Redwood Burn Limited, Trowbridge, Wiltshire
for David & Charles Publishers plc
Brunel House   Newton Abbot   Devon

Cover Pictures
Front: A 'fen tiger' out punt-gunning.
Back: Siberia Bewick swans on the fenland washes.
(Both pictures courtesy of Dave Parfitt.)

Contents

To my father-in-law, Ernie James

1

Welney in the Early Days

I was born on 8 January 1906 in the small Fenland village of Welney in south-west Norfolk, thirteen miles from Wisbech and ten from Ely. The cottage in which I was born stood on the high bank between two rivers, the Delph and the Old Bedford, and had belonged to my family for generations. It was known as the 'Ferry House' because my father, like his grandfather before him, operated the ferry across the washes during the winter when the main Wisbech to Ely road was flooded.

Anyone visiting Welney for the first time would probably get the impression of a long, straggling village, a mixture of old and new houses, some set back from the road and others built on the banks of the Old Bedford river. The main Wisbech to Ely road runs straight through the village and has two offshoots, Chestnut Avenue and New Road, which leads to March, about ten miles away. Hiding behind some sycamore trees in the main street is St Mary's, the nineteenth-century church; close by is the typical village school whose outward appearance is unmistakeably Victorian; and on the opposite side of the road stands the village shop which has changed little in my life-time. The old cabinets and shelves are still there, but today they are all stocked with pre-packaged foods. No longer do we have to wait patiently whilst the shopkeeper weighs out a pound of sugar from a large sack standing on the floor, deftly makes a cone-shaped bag out of a square of blue paper and pours the sugar into it, or perhaps cuts a pound of butter from a large slab on the counter and neatly wraps it in greaseproof paper, chatting to his customers all the while, repeating the latest village gossip. Now when I go into the shop everything is stacked on the shelves in orderly rows, ready to be sold in neat packages and brightly labelled cans, or stored in the frozen food cabinet by the door. In spite of these and other changes, however, the old atmosphere still seems to persist and I enjoy going to the shop to exchange a few words and have a laugh and joke with Ethel who owns the store today.

The village also had, until recently, its own bicycle shop with two petrol pumps standing outside to cater for the local people who own cars; but competition from garages in nearby villages forced it to close down. It has since been replaced by a craft shop which sells basket-ware, leather goods, pottery, jewellery and soft toys to the tourists who visit Welney. We still have our own post office, although it has moved from its original site in main street to New Road. It supplies anything from stamps, groceries and knitting wool, to fishing lines, rods and maggots.

Most of the social life in the village is centred on the village hall and pubs, frequented not only by local people but also by all the visitors who regularly come to Welney. In the summertime they come to enjoy some peaceful fishing or bird-watching and at the end of the day they generally go to the Lamb and Flag or the Three Tuns for a quiet drink, a chat with the locals, or a game of dominoes. In wintertime it is the wildfowlers who dominate the conversation in the pubs. They come in after a day's shooting and gather round the fires warming themselves, exchanging stories and comparing notes. During the shooting season the washes surrounding Welney are a popular hunting ground for wildfowlers and the noise of their guns can be heard from morning to night, especially at weekends.

Dissecting the village are three rivers running parallel and bounded by high banks. These rivers, the Old and New Bedford and the Delph, were the brainchild of Cornelius Vermuyden, a Dutch engineer invited to England in 1631 by the Fourth Earl of Bedford and a company of other men who undertook to reclaim the Fens. It was a huge task and Vermuyden devoted the rest of his life to it, assisted by Dutch labourers brought to Norfolk especially to do the job. It is said that such was his enthusiasm for the project that he invested much of his own money in the scheme and as a result died almost penniless.

There are four main rivers which flow through the Fens: the Great Ouse, Witham, Welland and Nene. They all collect water from large areas of uplands and flow down at a fairly steep gradient until they reach the wide, level plain of the Fens. When there was a flood, the water spread over the plain and turned it into a huge lake. This was the problem which faced Vermuyden. He concentrated his efforts on the Great Ouse and solved the dilemma by diverting half the waters of the river which drain down from Northamptonshire as far as Earith, along a different route to the sea. He built a sluice at Earith and cut two new rivers, the Old and New Bedford which run in a straight line, parallel to each other, from Earith to Denver, with flood banks to the east and west. Between these banks are about three-quarters of a mile of washlands which fill up when there is a flood. These two rivers run through Welney. The first one to be cut was the Old Bedford in 1637; it flows side by side with another river, the Delph, cut in 1657, and they are separated only by a high bank. The New Bedford, cut in 1642, is about three-quarters of a mile from the main part of the village. It is always known locally as the Hundred Foot because when Vermuyden cut this river it was one hundred feet in breadth with banks on either side sixty feet wide at the bottom, ten feet wide at the top, and eight feet high. Over the years the banks have had to be raised to their original height many times because the land is very peaty and therefore has a tendency to sink. The Hundred Foot was once spanned by a suspension bridge but this was replaced about sixty years ago by a new bridge, although the cluster of old cottages by the side of the bridge are still known as 'the houses at Suspension Bridge'. When I was a lad there were enough children living in those cottages to support a school there, but it has long since disappeared. Today the children who live near Suspension Bridge go to the school in Littleport, a large village about six miles away, midway between Welney and Ely.

If you follow the road running alongside the Hundred Foot eastwards from Suspension Bridge to the village of Ten Mile, you come to the Welney Wildfowl Refuge which was set up in 1968 and until recently was run by Josh Scott, an old friend of mine. Visitors come here from all over the world to see the ducks, geese and other rare birds which gather here every winter to feed. It is wonderful, especially on a dark winter's night, to sit in the observation cabin and look out over the washes, floodlit by huge spotlights, and watch all the Bewick swans, widgeon, teal, shovellers and pintails come flocking in when they catch sight of the warden pushing his barrowful of corn which he scatters on the edge of the water. There is a constant gaggle of noise as the birds duck and dive in search of their supper.

Welney is situated right in the middle of the Fens — a word which conjures up for most people a picture of bleakness. A vast area of treeless, flat land, damp and cold in winter and shrouded in a mist which years ago was reputed to be the cause of 'Fenland Ague', a disease suffered by many of the inhabitants of this area, the main symptom being painfully aching bones and joints.

Famous visitors to the Fens in the past have recorded their impressions and commented on the mists and dampness. Daniel Defoe wrote in his diary, 'The Fens appear covered with water, so too I observed that they generally at this latter part of the year also appear covered with fogs.' He also described Ely, commenting that: 'The Isle of Ely looked as if wrapped in blankets' and 'The people had no other breath to draw than that what must be mixed with these vapours and that steam which so universally overspread the country.'

Samuel Pepys, when he visited the Fens a century earlier thought them 'A heathen place' and he described his journey along 'Dikes where sometimes we were ready to have our horses sink to the belly.'

In wintertime it is true that the Fens are bleak. Welney is often surrounded by acres of flooded washes as far as the eye can see, and the wind can blow and howl with a terrible force, creasing the surface of the water into millions of tiny waves and flattening down any exposed grasses. If you look closely, however, the impression changes, because in reality the washes are a sanctuary for all kinds of wildlife. Each winter thousands of wildfowl come here to feed and you can see them silhouetted against the vast expanse of the sky, as they wheel and turn, soar and dive in their search for food. To me all the wildness and desolation, the great, flat expanses of water and sky, spell peace and tranquillity. When I go out in my boat, along the rivers or across the flooded washes, I want no other company save that of the birds around me.

Today I live with my wife in a small whitewashed cottage on the banks of the Old Bedford river about three hundred yards from Welney Bridge. In common with most Fenmen of my era and our forefathers before us, I never had a regular job. I lived by the seasons and chiefly earned my living out of perhaps a square mile of land, each job dovetailing into another. In the springtime there was willow-cutting and eel-catching. This was followed in the summertime by ditching in the washes and harvest work. Autumn saw the start of plover-catching which continued until the frost came, when we would be punt-gunning for wildfowl until spring.

I learned my various trades as a young boy by accompanying the old Fen characters who lived in Welney when they went out punt-gunning, plover-catching or eel-trapping. I watched what they did and listened to men like my father Alfred James or his friend Will Kent. They had a rich and fascinating store of knowledge about the Fens and the creatures who inhabit them, handed down by their forefathers. I remember my father and Will going off together to set their eel traps in the river. They generally worked a mile or so apart along the banks but they still managed to talk to each other as they worked because they knew that water carries sound. They did not need CBs or telephones to communicate with each other — they just shouted along the river!

2
School Days

When I was five I started attending the village school. In those days there were about eighty children at the school and two teachers. The younger pupils were taught by a Miss Patell, but my memories of her are vague; I remember only that she used to lodge with my aunt, Mrs Stovell, who lived in a house on the banks of the Old Bedford river. The schoolmaster in charge of the older children was Mr Bearcock and I'll never forget him. I can picture him now: a tall, stern, white-haired man with a large, white moustache. He was a tyrant and we were all terrified of him because he used to cane us most mornings whether we deserved it or not — it was his way of starting the day. A bachelor, he lived in the schoolhouse with his niece, who in addition to acting as his housekeeper also helped in the school sometimes. She was as bad as her uncle and frequently rapped our knuckles or pulled our hair. The end of the school day always came as a relief to everyone, including Mr Bearcock I think, because as soon as he had dismissed us he could be seen, white pitcher in his hand, dashing across the road to the Lamb and Flag for his daily ration of ale.

Schooling never did agree with me, and I used to learn more on my way to school than I did when I got there. I liked to watch the birds on the rivers and in the hedgerows or wheeling about in the sky, and by observation I learnt to identify them by their flight patterns. With other boys I played by the sides of the rivers, fished with homemade rods and in the springtime collected frog spawn, which unfortunately is not found around here anymore because the frogs have long since disappeared from these rivers.

In wintertime, when it was icy, the washes and rivers became huge skating rinks, and as children we all learnt to skate so that we could enjoy the pleasures they offered. If we knew that the rivers were frozen we needed no extra encouragement to climb out of bed, even though the mornings were bitterly cold and our bedrooms felt like ice-boxes. My brother and I used to get up as soon as mother called us, hurry downstairs to dress by the warmth of a blazing fire, eat our breakfast as quickly as we could and then dash down to the Old Croft river where we were joined by all our school mates. For a short time school was forgotten as we skated backwards and forwards on the ice, thoroughly enjoying ourselves. Suddenly, the school bell would ring out reminding us that it was nine o'clock and we all raced for the school gates, where Mr Bearcock was always waiting with a cane in his hand, ready to catch each of us as we passed through.

The school day started every morning with assembly; Mr Bearcock played the harmonium whilst we sang hymns. If he heard anyone singing out of tune he stopped playing to give them a smack across the ear. I used to try to sing very softly so that he could not hear me! After we had sung a hymn we had to kneel on the hard wooden floor to say our prayers. Although it was very uncomfortable we dared not shuffle about because if Mr Bearcock heard us moving he was soon after us. Assembly was followed by scripture, sums, reading and writing. The older children wrote in books but the young ones used slates. We all hated and dreaded sums, because the schoolmaster generally gave us a stroke of the cane for every sum we got wrong. There was one boy in my class by the name of Johnnie Singleterry who was hopeless at sums and always qualified for several strokes of the cane each day. Mr Bearcock used to repeat his name 'John-nie-Single-terry, John-nie-Single-terry', as he beat a rhythm out on the poor boy's hand with his stick.

I remember one particular morning when one of the older boys, much to his dismay, got nearly all his sums

As soon as he dismissed us Mr Bearcock was to be seen dashing across to the Lamb and Flag for his daily ration of ale

wrong. Mr Bearcock, looking down his nose as usual with a stern expression on his face, called the boy out and stood him in front of his desk. He then produced his cane and flexed it once or twice before proceeding to give the poor boy the appropriate number of strokes across his hand, counting out aloud as he did so, 'One, two, three, four, five.' When he reached the count of six or seven he said to the lad, 'Tell me when you've had enough boy.' But the lad was so terrified that he did not hear him; he just stood there trembling and holding out his hand. His friend who was sitting on the front row heard what Bearcock said and, anxious to save the boy from further punishment, whispered, 'Say you've had enough.'

The schoolmaster overheard him and immediately turned on the other boy, dragged him out to the front of the class and started caning him instead. Finally, something seemed to snap and both boys turned on old Bearcock simultaneously. One jumped onto his back and the other pulled his knitted tie tight around his neck. The rest of us were petrified; we watched open-mouthed and in complete silence, quite sure that they were trying to murder him and most of us secretly hoping that they would succeed. After what seemed like an eternity, but in fact would only be about a minute or two, both boys seemed to suddenly come to their senses, and, realising the error of their ways, lost their nerve and ran out of the classroom. The irate schoolmaster, red in the face and hot on their heels, chased them round and round the school yard but didn't manage to catch them. Eventually he returned to the classroom, his face like thunder, puffing and panting like an old steam engine. One of the troublemakers trailed into the classroom after him and sidled back to his seat with his head down where he remained very subdued for the rest of the day. He was obviously frightened because he kept his eyes down on his desk and didn't say a word to any of his friends. The other boy showed less courage because he ran off home and did not come back until the following day. The rest of us waited anxiously all that day to see what was going to happen, but, strangely, nothing did. The two boys were not punished in any way and the incident was never referred to again. One of those lads, Harry Kent, is still alive today at the age of eighty-four. He lives in Welney, close to the post office in New Road.

After school in the wintertime, when the wash road was often flooded for weeks at a time, I had to help my father ferry passengers backwards and forwards between the village and Suspension Bridge. Every Friday afternoon, as soon as school was finished, Mr Bearcock used to cycle to Ely, where he spent the weekend with his relatives who lived there. One Friday morning before I left for school, father told me that he was going out for the day, and as the washes were flooded I would have to row Mr Bearcock and his bicycle over to Suspension Bridge. Sometime, during lessons that day, I did something which upset old Bearcock; I can't remember now what it was, but he thought I deserved some punishment. Instead of caning me as he usually did, he told me to stay in after school and write out a hundred lines. Although I knew that he would want to be away to Ely as soon as school was over, I dared not open my mouth to tell him that I was the one who was ferrying him to Suspension Bridge that night. I just stayed behind when he dismissed everyone else and started to write out my lines. After a few minutes Mr Bearcock came storming back into the classroom and, pointing his finger at me, snarled, 'Put that away now, you can go!' He had gone to my house expecting father to be waiting there to row him across the washes, but when my mother told him that father was out he realised that he could not get to Ely without me, and so he had to come back and let me out of school!

I always had jobs to do on my father's smallholding when school was over for the day. We kept about twenty pigs which we fattened up for market, and my first job on arriving home was to feed them. I used to go to the mangel heap, collect a barrow-load of mangels and clean them before feeding them to the pigs along with the pig swill which I mixed up in a big tub.

When young piglets were born my father used to 'tosh' them. This meant that he broke off their teeth to prevent them from biting their mother when she suckled them. One day he told me to go into the sty where the old sow was happily nursing several newly-born piglets, and bring them out one at a time so that he could tosh them. I was not very keen to do it because I knew how temperamental sows could be when suckling their young, but I had to do as I was told. I dared not say 'No' to my father. I climbed cautiously over the fence and into the sty, crept forward and grabbed one of the young pigs, but the old sow turned and saw me and made a move as if to attack. I ran away as fast as I could and in my haste to get out of the sty I fell backwards over the fence, dropping the poor piglet, which was crying with fright. I picked myself up and stood there gasping for breath whilst inside the sty the old sow was grunting and snorting and the piglets, unhappy at being disturbed, were squealing for their mother. One of my father's friends, Ernie Moxon, happened to be visiting at the time and he leant on the fence, watching what was going on, thoroughly enjoying the spectacle. He burst out laughing when he saw me dive out of the sty and said, 'You know what your trouble is, don't you? You're scared of them, my old bor.'

Privately I had to agree with him, but I was not prepared to admit it. Pretending to be angry but really feeling very embarrassed I said, 'If you think it's so funny why don't you have a go?' Much to my surprise he replied, 'That old sow don't worry me none, give her a minute or two to settle herself down and I'll show you.'

And sure enough, as soon as she had quietened down, he climbed the fence, boasting over his shoulder as he went, 'You just watch me, bor, and you'll learn how it's done.'

Wasting no time he jumped down into the sty. As soon as the old sow heard him she turned round and stared, but did not make any move towards him. Ernie, however, must have read some sort of message in that look, because

*I fell backwards out of the sty, dropping the
young piglet as I went*

he didn't wait to discover what her next move would be. He dashed back to the fence like a streak of lightning and, in his hurry to climb over it missed his footing, slipped and fell over on the other side, just as I had done. Poor Ernie; he lay there on his back, legs in the air, speechless, whilst I stood over him gloating, laughing my head off. 'Who's not afraid of old sows now then?' I asked.

When father had fattened his pigs up to eight or nine stones, he sent for Billy Sutton, the local butcher, who killed them by slitting their throats. He then cleaned them and hung them ready to go to Smithfield market in London. I remember going off to school one morning at ten to nine, and when I came back for my lunch I counted eleven pigs hanging in the shed which Billy had slaughtered, dressed and hung whilst I had been at school — that's not bad for a morning's work.

When I was a lad I always looked forward to weekends and holidays when there was no school and no Mr Bearcock. Most Saturdays I visited Will Kent, my father's old friend; he fascinated me and I listened for hours to the stories he had to tell about the old Fen characters he knew when he was a lad. It was Will who first encouraged me to appreciate the beauty and solitude of the Fens, and through him I learnt to discover the haunts and habits of all the wildlife around me, which I had previously taken for granted. He was also the first person to introduce me to the thrill of wildfowling and plover-catching.

When I wasn't visiting Will on Saturdays I sometimes went to my father's basket-making shop which was on the main street about a hundred yards from the bridge. I liked to hang around watching his men at work, and it was not long before I learnt how to make baskets myself. Later my father taught me how to make eel-traps, and when I had made one or two he showed me how to set them in the rivers and catch eels, something I still enjoy doing to this day.

Another of my favourite pastimes was fishing. My father owned half a mile of private water in the river Delph and I used to go down there with my friend, Georgie Butcher. Using homemade rods, we managed to catch all kinds of fish: pike, roach and tench to name but a few. Twice a year I helped my father to drag the river and we usually reaped a real harvest of fish, which were packed into boxes and transported by horse and cart to Manea station for despatch to London and Billingsgate Market. Now it is illegal to drag the rivers because they are all controlled by the Anglian Water Authority.

In 1912 we had a sturgeon in the river Delph. It swam in at Wellmore Sluice from the Great Ouse but could not swim out again, because there was insufficient water in the river to allow it to turn. It was stuck about a mile from the sluice and Georgie and I, along with a crowd of other children, went to see it after school. Poor old thing; it lay there obviously exhausted by its attempts to swim round. Some of the old boys were standing on the banks at either side of the river armed with nets which they used to try and push the sturgeon round, but they could not budge it. After much discussion and argument, there were still no practical suggestions for moving the fish, so it was decided that the best thing to do would be to shoot it to put it out of its misery. Several of the old men had their guns with them and they all had a go at shooting it without success. In the end, someone suggested sending for Joey Butcher, Georgie's father, because he was a good shot with his old muzzle-loading gun. When Joey arrived he got the others to put a net underneath the fish to raise its head out of the water whilst he loaded his gun with ball bearings. When everything was ready he took aim and fired, killing the fish with his first shot. Everybody helped to drag it out of the river and on to the bank where it was weighed and found to be 34 stones. It was decided to send it to a fish merchant in London who gave such a good price for it that the men stayed away from work for a week and went on the booze with the money.

Georgie Butcher and I were good mates. We were about the same age and spent nearly all our spare time together.

When we got tired of fishing in the Delph we wandered along the banks, looking out for the marks of some animal or bird. There were all kinds of interesting things to see. We learnt to recognise the tracks made by otters, rabbits, hares and all kinds of vermin, and followed them to see where they led. One of our favourite pastimes was tracking birds and animals in the snow, because their footprints were so easy to identify in the soft white covering. Otters were recognisable, because apart from their footprints their tails left a trail mark where they had dragged along the ground.

We spent hours bird-watching. So many different species of birds came to Welney every year, and still do now, so it was always fun to go bird-watching either along the river banks or in the washes. In addition to all the wildfowl, we saw birds like kingfishers, bitterns, curlews and grebe. In springtime we knew where most of the nests were, how many eggs were in them and approximately when they were due to hatch. We enjoyed watching mother birds teaching their young ones how to fly, or the processions of ducklings swimming along behind their mothers. Sadly many of them did not survive for long. They were killed by either pike or rats and dragged under the water to be eaten. Today the young ducklings face an additional danger from mink, which roam wild in these parts.

Most of the children in Welney learnt to swim when they were about five years old. It was essential to learn early with three rivers flowing through the village. The older boys swam in the Delph and when the younger ones went down to watch they were sometimes thrown in — it was the quickest way to learn how to swim — but the older ones were always on hand to rescue any child who got into difficulties. Fortunately it was very rare that a child drowned in Welney, because we were all taught by our parents from a very early age to respect the rivers and be aware of their potential dangers.

Georgie and I did not spend all our time studying nature

or indulging in innocent country pursuits; in fact we always seemed to be in trouble as a result of our escapades. When it was dark, in wintertime, we would creep along a row of houses tying door knobs together, then knock at the doors and run away to hide, making sure that we had a good view of what was happening from our hiding place. After a minute or two one door opened, and then another, but as the second door opened the first would be forced to close, and a kind of tug-of-war developed as neighbours tried to keep their doors open so that they could untie the ropes which held them together. Sometimes, instead of tying two door knobs together, we'd carve up a mangel in the shape of an old man's head, fix it to the top of a stake and then put a lighted candle inside it. We leant it against a door, knocked, and then ran away. When someone came to answer our knock they usually got a terrible fright and the old women often screamed, especially if the mangel fell inside the door. On reflection, it was a stupid and dangerous trick to play as we could have set the house on fire.

One night Georgie and I went to the Institute. This was a room above the parson's stable which he allowed us to use as a reading room. Whilst we were there some of the older boys started to tease Georgie and generally mess him about, so he said to me, 'Come on, I've had enough. Let's go home.'

As we walked away from the vicarage Georgie said,
'I've done them tonight.'
'What are you on about?' I asked.
'I've locked them in.' I laughed and said, 'What have you done with the key?'
'I've thrown it away,' was Georgie's reply.
We said no more about it, and parted on the bridge to go our different ways home. As I walked on I thought to myself 'We haven't heard the last of this; I bet there'll be trouble later.'

I was right. There was a dreadful row, because not only were the boys locked in but also some of the older men, including the postman and the carpenter who had gone there for a quiet game of draughts. At first nothing happened. It was only when someone wanted to go home and could not open the door that the people inside realised that they were locked in. Everyone started shouting, but their cries were not heard for quite a long time and it was impossible to get out without help because the room was quite high up, over the stable block, and the only window was sited directly above the ash pit. Eventually, when it was close on midnight, the gardener at the parsonage went on his nightly round checking that everything was in order. Hearing cries coming from the reading room, he went to investigate and released everyone by unlocking the door with his spare key. Of course it did not take much imagination to guess who was the culprit, and because I had been with Georgie I was implicated too. The parson was furious, not just because Georgie had locked the men in, but also because so many wives and mothers had been worried, wondering what had happened to their menfolk. He went to Georgie's house the next day and told him to keep away from the Institute in future, as he would never be allowed in again.

There was a man who came to Welney regularly to empty the slot machines in the pubs. He rode on an old motor bike with a sidecar made of wicker. Whenever he came there was always a young boy with him riding as his passenger, who was his son. He had to visit the three pubs in the village and two more over the washes at Suspension Bridge. When there was water on the wash road he left his motor bike on top of the bridge in the care of the little boy, and went over the washes in my father's boat. Georgie and I often chatted to the lad whilst he was hanging about waiting for the man to return and it did not take us long to realise that he was easy to handle and would fall in with any suggestions we made. One day, as we were all three standing on the bridge watching my father's boat disappear across the flooded washes with his passenger on board, Georgie turned to me and said, 'How do you fancy a ride on the motor bike?'

I thought that it was a great idea, and it did not take us long to persuade the boy to let us have a ride, assuring him that the bike would be quite safe with us. We got on the bike and roared up and down the street having a wonderful time, gaining confidence and speed with every minute. Suddenly, disaster struck! The nose of the sidecar hit one of the pillars supporting the bridge and it was smashed to bits, pieces of wicker flying in all directions and tokens from the slot machines rolling all over the road. 'That's corped it,' said the lad in a horrified voice. We looked at the shattered sidecar in dismay and had to agree with him. Trying to salvage what we could, we got on our hands and knees in the roadway and, helped by the lad, tried to gather up all the scattered tokens, hastily stuffing them into the remains of the sidecar. But of course we kept a few back for ourselves because we knew that we could exchange them at the pub and buy some cigarettes to smoke behind the hedge. As soon as all the tokens were gathered up Georgie and I took ourselves off and kept well out of sight until we knew that the slot machine man and his motor bike were several miles away from Welney.

Another of my father's regular passengers was the grocery man, who came each week to deliver goods to Welney shop and Jackson's grocery store near Suspension Bridge. He came in an old Ford T car. My uncle owned a similar model and he taught me how to start his car. He explained how the various parts of the engine worked, and I was quite confident that I would be able to drive the grocery man's car if I ever got the chance. One day Georgie and I spotted the car parked on the bridge with no one near it. It was an opportunity too good to miss and after checking that my father and his passenger were out of sight across the washes, we turned to the car. Georgie said, 'I bet I can crank that old Ford up more times than you can.' (There were no self starters then.)

'I bet you can't,' said I, rising to the challenge.

'Right, I'll have a go first,' said Georgie, as he picked up the starting handle.

We looked in dismay at the shattered sidecar

I counted as he cranked. When he was exhausted he gasped, 'Now it's your turn, you have a go.'

I took the starting handle from him and bent down to start cranking, never suspecting that Georgie was up to something. But as soon as my back was turned, he switched on the engine and pulled the throttle which was located just beneath the steering wheel. The engine immediately roared into life, frightening me to death. I stopped cranking, panicked and ran to the top of the bridge to see if there was any sign of the ferry boat returning. Sure enough, there was my father and the grocery man approaching the bank and it was quite obvious that they had heard the row. As soon as they saw us they guessed that we had been up to some mischief with the car and one look at their faces told us to disappear fast, so we went and hid in the shed at the back of the Lamb and Flag to allow my father's temper to cool a little. When he eventually caught up with me I still got into terrible trouble, and looking back deserved it, because had the car been in gear it could have careered away on its own and run into something. We were just fortunate that no damage was done.

Uncle Harry Stovell was my father's sister's husband; my aunt and he lived in London where he used to drive a cab. When my paternal grandfather died my aunt and uncle came to live in Welney so that my aunt could take over the running of the village store, which had belonged to my father's family for generations. Uncle Harry got a job with the post office when he arrived in Welney. He drove the mail-cart from Wisbech to Welney each day to bring us our letters and parcels.

After a time the post office pensioned off all their horses and uncle Harry was asked to drive a mail-van instead. As he had never driven one before he took lessons from Harry Kent, one of the local men. Poor uncle Harry! He was a hopeless driver and used to have an accident nearly every day. Harry Kent tried to help by offering to give him some more lessons and it was agreed that they should meet one afternoon in the yard at the back of the Lamb and Flag for the first of these. I went along to watch. Harry Kent had already parked the van outside the back door and he was just telling my uncle how he should drive the van slowly and carefully round to the front, when I arrived. Now, to get from the back to the front of the pub in those days, you had to go through an archway, and Harry Kent warned uncle Harry that he had to be particularly careful when he came to the archway. He told him to drive the van very slowly and steadily through it. My uncle nodded his head in agreement, got into the van and started it. When he switched on the ignition, the engine seemed to explode into life and the van set off like a bat out of hell, swerving wildly about the yard with uncle Harry clinging desperately to the steering wheel. He flashed by me like a streak of lightning; I flattened myself against the wall and the van came to rest violently, rammed up against the archway with both its headlights bashed in. Harry Kent and I leant against each other, tears streaming down our cheeks and helpless with laughter. Poor uncle Harry; as far as the post office was concerned it was the last straw, just one accident too many, because it was costing them a fortune for his repair bills. His van was taken away and he was made village postman instead. They thought that he was much safer on two legs than four wheels.

As the postman, uncle Harry did a lot of walking each day, because he had to deliver mail to cottages three or four miles along the Bedford Bank, as well as to the isolated farms in the Fens, and he had to go out in all weathers. One day, when the ice was bearing, uncle Harry had finished delivering his letters along the Bedford Bank and decided to walk back along the river instead of the bank, because he thought that it would be easier. As he strode confidently along the ice he did not realise that the Smart brothers, who lived two miles from Welney along the Bedford Bank, had been out the previous night and cut a channel across the river in order to take their boat to the other side. The channel was now frozen over again and the ice covered with a thin layer of snow. Suddenly uncle

Harry fell straight through the thin ice, up to his neck in icy water. Fortunately he was not far from the bank and he managed to struggle out to safety, but he was very cold, soaking wet and about two miles from home. He set off and ran down the bank as fast as he could, to the warmth of a good fire and the comfort of the large glass of whisky which he knew would be waiting at home.

Wisbech was our local market town, and when I was a lad the only way to get there was by horse and trap because there were no buses in those days. A man called Arthur Wintass, who lived in Welney, used to take his horse and trap to Wisbech, thirteen miles away, every Saturday. He was able to carry four passengers in the trap with him and he charged them half-a-crown (twelve-and-a-half pence) for the return journey. Two of the passengers sat in the front with Arthur and two behind, back to back. They always had a good gossip on the way, because it took a fair time to get there. My father liked to go most Saturdays, so on Friday nights he would say to me, 'Go and see Arthur Wintass and ask if I can go to Wisbech with him tomorrow.'

Sometimes I was allowed to accompany him, usually when I needed some new clothes. I loved going, because there was always so much to see. I followed my father around the shops, acting as his porter and carrying his parcels. We usually stayed about three or four hours and had lunch in a restaurant, but occasionally, if it was a nice day, we bought a pork pie each and ate it outside. I remember those pork pies; they tasted delicious. After we had finished them we went to the pub for a drink and whilst my father was in the bar, I was allowed to sit in a room at the back with a glass of lemonade: I loved it.

On the way home Arthur always stopped at a pub in Outwell, midway between Welney and Wisbech and called, appropriately, The Half Way House. This was the one bit of the excursion that I hated, because I had to sit in the cart waiting whilst Arthur and my father disappeared through the door of the pub. I knew that I would not see them again for perhaps an hour or two. It always seemed worse in wintertime when darkness fell early and there was a frost in the air. They seemed to be gone twice as long as they actually were, and I sat huddled up in the cart, frozen stiff, watching the door open and close and willing my father to appear each time, and say that he was ready for home.

Wisbech Mart was held on the first and second Saturday in March each year. It was very popular and people from all the surrounding villages used to flock there to enjoy all the amusements and diversions. As far as I was concerned though the highlight of the year was Welney Feast Day, 18 June, the start of our annual village fair. Fairground people came year after year and set up their stalls, which stretched the length of the street from Welney bridge to the rectory. They generally came from Downham Market which held a fair the week before our fair. Many of the travelling families arrived in the morning, set up their stalls and then retired to the pubs until early in the evening when the fair officially opened. There was a real carnival atmosphere in the village that night. People dressed up in their best clothes and for most of the men it was the start of a week's holiday, so they were in the mood to enjoy all the fun the fair offered. It was guaranteed that there would be something for everyone: swings, roundabouts, cake walks, coconut shies, hoop-la stalls and fortune-tellers, who were always very popular. A fiddler came from somewhere in Norfolk each year to entertain us. He arrived for the start of the feast and stayed on for a week, playing all day long in the pubs. In the evenings the men crowded into the bars and danced to the music of the fiddler, whilst the women were left at home looking after the children. In those days they were not welcome in the pubs; a woman's place was definitely thought to be in the home.

I can remember now the feeling of sadness and emptiness I experienced every time I saw the travelling folk packing up at the end of the fair and moving out of the village. There was always a sense of anticlimax and life seemed very dull for a day or two afterwards.

Georgie and I were both fond of music and we learnt to play various instruments whilst still at school. Every Sunday night after church I went with my mother to visit an old lady in the village called Amelia Snelling. She was a kind old soul and I enjoyed going to see her because she had an accordian which she taught me to play. When she thought that I could play it reasonably well she gave it to me, saying that I would get more pleasure from it than she did.

I also learnt how to play the violin; I taught myself to play on my father's instrument which he allowed me to practise on. Later I bought one of my own from a man called Mr Littleproud who lived in Upwell. I was very proud of that violin because Mr Littleproud had been a fiddler in the army during World War I and he had carried it all through the war with him.

Georgie learnt to play the piano and accordian and we spent many happy hours together, playing all the old songs and singing at the tops of our voices. We thought that we played very well and could not understand why our talents were not appreciated at home, where the sight of our accordians and my violin brought loud moans and protests from friends and relations. In fact, when I pick up the old violin and accordian now for the odd tune or two, I still get the same reaction from my family as I did all those years ago. Everyone retires to another room or my wife suggests that I take my instruments and myself off to my shed where I can amuse myself without disturbing other people. No one seems to enjoy my playing except of course me!

I often think back to those days of my youth and compare them with the lifestyle of the youngsters today. They have their cars and motor bikes and can travel from one end of the country to the other. They have their transistors, videos, computers, clubs and sports facilities. So much seems to be provided for them and yet I am sure they do not get as much pleasure from life today as we did from our more leisurely, simple, pursuits years ago.

3
Work and Play

During World War I labour was very scarce because all the able-bodied men were away fighting, and the ones left behind had to do the work of three or four men. My father had a smallholding in Welney, and towards the end of the war, when I was twelve, he obtained special permission for me to leave school so that I could help him on the land. I was glad to leave, but found the new work very hard because I was expected to turn my hand to all kinds of jobs which were normally done by fully grown men. We kept a couple of horses for pulling the plough and carting the corn, and I had to feed them and muck them out each day.

The smallholding provided us with a steady income, but our main business was osier growing. My father had three or four acres of osier beds which he had inherited from his father-in-law, who had paid £200 an acre for them more than a hundred years before — that was a lot of money then! At first, he sold all his willows to local basket-makers in Ely, King's Lynn, Manea and Wisbech. He had an arrangement with one of them in Ely whereby, instead of receiving a cash payment, he supplied his customer with so many bundles of rods in exchange for four or five dozen potato baskets. When the rods had been cut I used to harness one of the horses to a four-wheeled trolley, load it up with willows and take them into Ely. When I returned to Welney I had a trolley-load of baskets. After a time father decided it would be a good idea to employ his own basket-makers, and he set on two men to produce baskets for him. The first one was John Burton, who came from Haddenham, and father supplied him with a house in the village. He worked for us for several years before leaving to set up his own business, but unfortunately he was a better basket-maker than businessman; he soon ran into difficulties and had to give up and return to Haddenham. Our other basket-maker, also called John, worked for us for a long time. He lodged at the Cherry Tree, where he was popular with all the customers because he was a real character and full of fun. There was a half-door in the basket-making shop and the local children liked to hang over it to watch the men at work inside. If John had an audience when he was cutting the osiers he would flick the rods over so that they landed on the door. This soon made the children jump out of the way as John called out, teasing them, 'Don't worry; you can stay there, you are not in my way!'

One day John met me as I was returning from a day's shooting in the washes. I was carrying a few ducks I had bagged over my shoulder, and he said, 'I'll have one of those from you.'

He paid me and took it home to Mrs Smith, his landlady at the Cherry Tree, who cooked it for him. The following day he saw me passing the shop and called out, 'That duck of yours was a good 'un. I really enjoyed it, I'll have another one from you sometime.'

Two weeks later he met me on the bridge and said, 'I'm ready for another duck, but this time I'm going to pick it myself.'

At first I thought that he wanted to choose one, but he continued, 'Old Mrs Smith charged me ninepence for picking that other one and I reckon I can pick my own and save ninepence.' I realised then that he meant pluck it when he said pick it. I supplied him with a nice duck, but I heard afterwards that he had made such a mess of plucking it that Mrs Smith had difficulty in cooking it. He certainly didn't offer to pluck anymore afterwards.

John's favourite hobby was horse racing. When there was a meeting coming up he used to say to father, 'Can I have a week off, Alf, please? They're racing at Newmarket next week and I want to go and see the gee-gees.'

If we were not too busy father allowed him to go, but he often came back before the end of the races if he had run out of money. When this happened he went straight round to see my father.

'Can you let me have a sub, Alf, please? I've backed a loser, but I'll be back at work again next week, so you'll get your money back.'

His fondness for horses was not matched by an ability to pick winners, consequently he was invariably in debt to my father after his trips to Newmarket.

One morning Harry Smith, the landlord of the Cherry Tree, came dashing up to the bridge to see my father, looking very upset. 'I've just been in to old John and he's dead,' he said. 'Well, that's a rum 'un,' replied my father, who was very shocked by the news, although John had suffered from chronic asthma for years and had had several bad attacks in the workshop. On the day of the funeral I stood on top of the bridge with old Charlie Rudland and his mates and we watched as they carried poor old John into the churchyard. There were only three followers; Harry Smith, the policeman and my father. As they walked through the church gate, the solemnity of the moment was broken by Charlie Rudland who laughed and remarked, 'I reckon the policeman must be suspicious of old John, the way he's following him into the churchyard like that.'

After the funeral father gave me old John's basket-making tools and I still think of him today when I am sitting in my shed using them myself.

Our busiest time of the year on the land was harvest-time. In my young days the corn was harvested by hand. We used a two-handled scythe with a long, straight blade attached to the shaft so that it curved inwards. The shaft was three or four feet long, with two kegs which acted as handles. Mowing was not an easy job, but I became expert at it because I was taught by some of the best men in the country. Even in those days only the old countrymen could mow properly. When I first started I quickly learnt the importance of setting the blade correctly. I was taught to stick out my toes, rest the shaft against my chest, and if I could just touch the end of the blade with my toe it was correctly set. Although the blade was straight, it had to be set at an angle so that when mowing, you were not catching the corn straight, but coming round all the while.

We always grew five or six acres of corn which we mowed by hand, and all the family had to help, young and old alike. In fact, at harvest-time, everyone in the village was involved in some way or another. If they didn't have any corn of their own to harvest they went to help someone else. The mower always went ahead to cut the corn and his helpers, usually his wife and elder children, followed, gathering up the swath with a tommy-hawk which looked like a reaper hook. They tied it into sheaves with corn bands made by the smaller children, and the sheaves were stacked into shocks — twelve sheaves in each shock. The corn was left standing like this until it was thoroughly dried out and then we loaded up a cart and took it away to be stacked. When the field was empty, the elder children went over it with harvest rakes, four or five feet wide, and raked up all the surface corn. After that the field was cleared, either by the gleaners with their corn sacks tied around their waists, who gathered up the remaining corn, or by chickens which were put into the field in coops to eat up the oddments. The gathered corn was threshed using an ordinary steam engine, drum and jack straw, which was like an elevator. Sometimes we left the corn sheeted down or thatched until the following spring before threshing it and taking it to Bennetts, the corn merchants in Downham Market, to be sold. We always kept a little corn back which we took to the windmill in the village where Mr Lowding, the miller, ground it up for pig food.

When I was small, my mother used to sit with me in the evenings when harvest was over and amuse me by telling stories about things which happened at harvest-time when she was young and had to help her father. My favourite story was about one of the local farmers who was mowing one day, helped by two or three of his sons. The work was not going at all well because his scythe would not cut the corn properly and he kept having to stop and sharpen it. He was puzzled and could not understand what was wrong. Finally, he paused, leant on his scythe, scratched his head and then happened to turn round just in time to see his lads with their hands full of small stones, which they were throwing into the standing corn. They knew that every time their father went through the corn with his scythe and hit the stones they would blunt his blade, so that he would have to stop and sharpen it, giving them time to have a rest. The farmer was furious when he realised what the boys had been up to and, taking off his belt, grabbed each one in turn and gave them a jolly good hiding.

I was mowing for my father one day helped by a man called Bill Johnson who was a typical Fenman. Although he was working some distance away from me I could see that he kept stopping and waving his arms about, apparently knocking flies from his face. A little while later I saw him run out into the middle of the field, take off his hat and throw it down, obviously in a temper, so I stopped working and went over to discover what was the matter.

'What on earth are you doing, Bill?' I asked.

'I've struck a wasp's nest and their feet are hot,' he replied.

'Well, what have you done with your hat?'

'I threw it at them,' he answered.

All the time we were talking he was waving his hands about like windmills, trying to sweep away the wasps which were still buzzing around his face. As his arms circled his head they accidentally caught his ears, knocking his glasses off; they flew into the air and landed somewhere in the corn. This final incident sent him into a terrible rage, because he could not see a thing without them. He stamped his feet and shouted and swore at the wasps whilst I got down on my hands and knees to search for his glasses — no easy task. Eventually I found them and gave them back to him, and his good humour returned as soon as he put them on his nose. Bill, still surrounded by wasps, went back into the corn with me quite happily to search for his hat which was still missing.

On another occasion Bill and I were working with several other men on a contract for the River Board, mowing grass off the banks. At the end of the day's work we all clambered into a small punt to cross the Old Bedford to collect our wages from the foreman of the River Board. We had not got very far from the bank when the boat started to sink because there were so many of us in it. One by one we all jumped out; everyone, that is, except Bill, who remained where he was in the boat, shouting, 'A captain should never desert a sinking ship!'

It was not long before the water was up to his neck and his dinner bag, which he was carrying round his shoulders, floated like a parachute on the water behind him. At that point he had the choice of abandoning ship or drowning. He decided that life was still worth living and struck out for the bankside, his face peeping out of the water and looking for all the world like a walrus.

One very hot day we were working on the banks about a quarter of a mile from the Welney Hotel when Bill suddenly disappeared.

'I bet he's gone to the hotel for a drink,' one of the men remarked.

Bill soon reappeared, sauntering along the top of the bank.

'Hello!' I shouted, 'enjoyed your pint of beer?'

'Beer!' exclaimed Bill, I've had no pints of beer, I had a drink out of the river instead.'
He never troubled about the dangers of pollution.

A few days later it was still very hot and one of the men offered Bill a drink of his home brewed beer.

'By, that's good,' said Bill after he had had a drink. 'I'll have to have a go at making some of that myself.'

As soon as he had finished work that night he went to

the village shop to buy a kit for brewing his own beer. He discovered that they had sold out of beer kits so he bought one for brewing stout instead, took it home and made it up straight away. The following morning when we were working together on opposite banks of the drain I shouted across to Bill, 'How did your beer making go?'

'I made two quarts,' he replied.

'Is that all? I thought you were supposed to make two gallons!'

He turned to his dinner bag, pulled out a quart bottle and threw it over the drain to me.

'Try that!' he shouted.

I took one mouthful and spat it out. It tasted dreadful.

'What's the matter; don't you like it?' he asked.

'Like it! It's as thick as tar!' I exclaimed. 'You should have added more water and left it to ferment.'

'You're too fussy; I could drink a barrel-full of it, if it wasn't for the smell,' he boasted, and with that he took the other bottle from his dinner bag and downed it straight away.

My father grew several acres of corn each year and at harvest-time he employed two or three casual labourers, in addition to my brother and myself, to mow his corn. As soon as it was cut, six of us went on to work for the commissioners of the River Board mowing the drains using long roding scythes with short blades and long shafts. We stood on top of the bank and reached right down with our scythes, seven or eight feet to the water, to mow the grass and wilt off the sides of the bank.

Next we had to shear the bottom of the drains, and we worked in pairs, one on each bank, using several blades bolted together. The number of blades depended upon the width of the drain. On each end of the blades was a chain which weighted them down, and ropes were attached to the chains with handles on the ends. You held the rope in both hands and jerked it; your partner on the opposite bank then jerked the rope from his side, thus producing an action similar to sawing wood with a cross saw. The six of us were contracted to cut the weeds in ten or twelve miles of drains and we managed to do about a mile a day. It was hard work; not many people were able to do it and we received a special bonus from the commissioners. Today I wish I had a pound note for every chain I'd cut: I would never need to do any more work, just talk about it! Now the drains are no longer mowed by hand. Weed cutters are used to clean the bottom of drains and the sides are sprayed with weed-killer.

I always welcomed the finish of all the mowing jobs, not just because it meant the end of some very hard work and long hours in the fields and on the banks, but because I knew that the next job which had to be done was the threshing, and this was my favourite. The threshing machine, and the old man who was in charge of it and drove it, fascinated me. The man's name was Doddy Rudland and he lived close by me. When I first started to help him he must have been about seventy years old and had a mop of lovely, clean, white, shining hair and always wore gold earrings. His eyesight was poor, and although he wore copper-rimmed glasses, they did not seem to help him much. Of course in those days no one went to an optician to have their eyes tested; they just went out and bought a pair of spectacles where they could. I spent a lot of time with Doddy, sitting up in the engine with him, asking countless questions which he answered very patiently because he knew how keen I was to know how everything worked. As he sat there with his head nodding he would say to me,

'How much steam have we got on, bor?'

'About fifty pounds,' I answered.

'You'd better put another shovel or two of coal on then, we mustn't let her run down; we've got to keep it up to about sixty or seventy pounds.'

It was easy to tell when the steam was running down because the engine started to cough. Doddy would listen, putting his head on one side and then shout to me, 'Put some more coal on, I know she's running back.'

I felt like a king when I was on that engine. I thought that it was marvellous sitting up there pulling the levers and blowing in the water pipe to see how much water there was in the glass. This had to be done in order to regulate the steam in the engine. As I grew a little older, Doddy allowed me to stop the engine at lunch time and re-start it again later, and that was the highlight of my day.

When I was about fourteen I started to carry water for the threshing machine and after a while I moved on to carrying the chaff away. As I grew older and stronger I was allowed to carry the corn which was very hard work. There was generally a gang of us working together and when we got really tired, one of us would go to the drum, knock a strap off and then run up to the engine driver and shout, 'The chaff is blocked, Doddy!'

Doddy was wise to all the tricks we got up to and he'd say, 'Ah! You've knocked that strap off agin!'

'No, we ain't touched it,' we lied.

Poor old Doddy had to stop the engine, climb down, stick his hand into the drum where the chaff was stuck and pull it down, because as soon as the strap was off, the chaff blocked the drum. Whilst he was doing this, we were able to sit down and have a little rest. When it was unblocked, off we would go again until we felt ready for another rest and then one of us would repeat our little act of sabotage. Sometimes the drum stopped of its own accord without any help from us, if, for example, the elevator strap came off, but it made no difference; we still got the blame.

Threshing was a very dirty job, especially if it was done in the springtime when the corn had been stored since the previous autumn. There was so much dust flying about when the corn was lifted up to the threshing machine that we were soon covered in it. I think that it was almost as dirty as being down a coal mine, because by the end of the day we were spitting black dust and it took us some time to completely clear our lungs. It really was terrible. Women were employed to carry the chaff away from the engine and they always had to wear goggles and something over their

42

mouths, because with so much dust flying about it was difficult to see and breathe. People just would not do it today and certainly not for the money we received. The men were paid six shillings a day (the equivalent of thirty pence), and the women only got three shillings (fifteen pence). Just imagine! That was all they earned for working in those conditions, but in those days they were always glad to do it.

When I was older I travelled around to different farms in the area with the threshing tackle. I usually carried the corn and fed the drum, but eventually I was allowed to move the engine and set it up. I have spent weeks with that threshing machine, and it is hard to believe that most youngsters today have never even seen one. We always had some fun when we were threshing, but I enjoyed it more when there was someone else with me, close to my age, to share in the mischief. If I misbehaved when I was with the threshing gang, one of the older men soon took off his belt and strapped me. I knew that I could not go home and complain to my parents, because I would have only been told that I deserved it and in all probability my father would have given me a few more strokes with his belt.

In 1927 the old suspension bridge was replaced and I helped to build the new one, which took about a year to complete. A Dutch firm was in charge of the construction and they employed about twenty local men as labourers. First we had to build the approach road at either side of the bridge, and we removed hundreds of tons of soil from the sides of the banks of the Hundred Foot river. Small railway lines were laid down, and, starting close to the bridge, we dug out the sides of the banks, making the Hundred Foot river about ten feet wider. (It soon silted up again and went back to its original width.) All the soil was loaded into trucks and horses pulled these along the railway tracks to the bridge, where the soil was unloaded. Thousands of truck loads of soil were needed to raise the road to the required height, and it took us weeks. Hard-core, brought in by lorries, was laid on top of the soil and then it was tarmaced. Whilst all this was going on, the old bridge was left standing to enable traffic to flow freely between Wisbech and Ely. The actual construction of the new bridge involved driving piles into the river-bed, making huge boxes and pouring wet concrete, reinforced with steel, into them. When the concrete had set, the boxes were removed and the supports for the bridge were in position. The arches of the bridge were also made of reinforced concrete.

When the wash road was flooded during the winter months, father and I had to ferry all the workmen over to Suspension Bridge. There were so many of them that we had to take two boats, father rowing one and me the other. Soon, encouraged by our passengers, we started racing over and it became a point of honour to reach the other side first, the workmen cheering us all the way across.

One member of the construction gang was an old Dutchman who had his own barge and pile driver. One lunchtime he asked us to help him turn his boat round in the river. It was not an ideal time to do it because the tide was right up and he knew, just as we did, that once the water had reached its full height it started to drop again very quickly — about a foot in the first quarter of an hour. I think that the old fellow was full of rum at the time, and if we had had any sense we would have persuaded him to wait for the rising tide, but we didn't and we began to turn the barge around slowly. Predictably, the water level fell rapidly and soon the boat was stuck right across the river, the ends resting on the bank at either side, with the middle section showing signs of sagging. There was nothing we could do about it and finally the hull snapped and broke up and the barge was beyond repair. It became nothing more than a collection of firewood which we gathered up and shared out to keep the home fires burning.

One day a photographer from Wisbech arrived to take photographs of the newly completed bridge and the men who had helped to construct it. He set his tripod up on the bridge, carefully placed his camera on the top and covered it with a large black cloth. We were all gathered together in front of the camera and the photographer pushed and jostled us about until we were arranged to his satisfaction, and then he disappeared under the black cloth behind the camera. Amongst the workmen was an old navvy by the name of Ike See. He was very popular locally and famed for the size of his ears. Just as the photographer was about to take the picture, one of the young lads stepped forward and tugged at his jacket. His head reappeared from beneath the cloth and, looking far from pleased, he snapped at the lad, 'What do you want?'

'I'm just a-wondering if you'll be able to get Ike's ears on,' he said, with a cheeky grin on his face.

Before the photographer could reply, Ike shouted, 'I may have big ears but at least they're clean; I do wash 'em. Yours ain't been washed for the last twelve months and I'm not going to have my picture took with you and your filthy ears.'

With that he stormed off. Some of us ran after him and tried to persuade him to come back, but it was no use; he was too upset. The others who stayed on the bridge turned angrily on the lad, telling him that he should have kept his mouth shut. The poor photographer meanwhile was running first to one group and then to the other, shouting and trying to get everyone to go back to their places. Eventually he managed to get us all together again and, after rearranging us once more, took the photograph. Ike See was not in it, however; he refused to have anything more to do with it.

When Georgie Butcher and I were old enough, we often met in the pub after a day's work. It was the social centre of the village as far as the men were concerned, and we used to sit in a corner listening to the old men telling yarns and reminiscing about their younger days. Georgie's father, Joey, was a master story-teller, and once he started he could entertain the other customers in the tap room all night. He had a fund of wonderful tales because he had a vivid imagination and was into everything. He made it his business to know what everyone in and around Welney was doing and he had done such a variety of jobs that he always had something to talk about.

When he was a youngster he had joined the militia and he always wore a broad leather belt, with a large shiny buckle, to remind himself and everyone else of those days. He was extremely proud of that belt and polished it regularly. Whenever he went to work, he took it off, and put it down where he knew it would be safe and he could keep an eye on it. Woebetide anyone who dared to touch it! When meeting somebody for the first time, he often boasted to them that he had cut off an Irishman's ear with the buckle. If he said it in my father's hearing, father would shout, 'Not you, Joey!'

'Oh but I did, Alf,' he insisted, and then would go on to describe how he had come across two Irishmen fighting. They were both big, strong fellows and, according to Joey, the fighting was so fierce that one of them was in danger of being killed. Several onlookers had tried to separate them without success, so Joey had stepped forward, taken off his belt and with just one stroke had caught one of the Irishmen on the side of his head and cut his ear clean off with the buckle. How much truth there was in that story I do not know!

During the wintertime when the river was frozen and Joey was unable to work outside, he knitted nets for my father or made eel-traps. Sometimes father allowed him to make a few for himself, and he sold some of these to Will Kent. Old Will was as cunning as a fox and he'd go to the pub, stand by Joey, buy him a few pints of beer and encourage him to talk. He appeared to be totally engrossed in what Joey was saying, his eyes never leaving his face and his head nodding in agreement at everything that was said. He knew that Joey loved an audience; it always put him in a good humour, and the more he talked the more he drank. Will waited until Joey had plenty of beer inside him, and then bought all his hives at a very low price, knowing that by this time Joey was feeling very kindly disposed towards him. Later, when he was setting the hives in the river he would put his spret into one of them, give it a good sharp shove, and say, 'Get you down there, Joey!'

Joey was also a great practical joker and loved to tease all the old men. One day he was standing on top of Welney Bridge talking to Cutty See, a very famous old speed-skater who had won the National Championship one year. As they stood chatting together an aeroplane flew over, and Joey turned to Cutty and said, 'Shut up, I'm listening,' and cocked his head on one side and cupped his hand round his ear, apparently concentrating very hard. A moment or two later he pointed to the aeroplane which was circling overhead and said to Cutty, 'Listen, that bloke's got his wireless on.'

Poor old Cutty stood on tiptoe, straining his neck, with his mouth wide open, trying to listen.

'I can't hear it,' he complained.

'Well you must be deaf then,' said Joey, as he walked away chuckling to himself.

Sometimes when I went up to Will Kent's house on Saturdays Joey accompanied me, because he was one of the favoured few who were encouraged to visit the Kents. Often Will was away at market and so at lunchtime Joey would draw up Will's chair to the table for his 'dockey', as he called his lunch. Each time Will's wife Maria invited him to 'have a bit of vittals, Joey,' he replied, 'Well I ain't hungry, but I might as well have a bit.' He then proceeded to eat twice as much as anyone else when Maria put the dinner on the table. After he had finished eating Maria always said to him, 'Are you going to have a glass of wine Joey?' 'Oh, I might as well have a drop,' he would say before downing a few glasses of Mrs Kent's homebrew. She always made her own wine each year and stored it in nine-gallon casks, where it was left to mature for at least twelve months before use. One day she went over to draw some wine for Joey and when she returned she remarked, 'I think its getting low, Joey, because it's starting to guggle.'

I sat there saying nothing but thinking to myself, 'I know why it begins to guggle.'

The previous week Maria's nephew, George Kent, and I had been dyking in the washes and had called at the Kent's cottage hoping for some refreshment because it was very hot. There was no one at home so we had gone in and helped ourselves to a fair amount of her wine. I didn't dare admit it to Mrs Kent, but I was the one who made the wine guggle!

In those days all the pubs in Welney were very crudely furnished. We sat on wooden benches at plain long wooden tables and there were spittoons on the floor filled with sawdust. If we ran out of topics for conversation there were always plenty of other things to amuse us because all the pubs provided games for their customers. There were ring boards in every tap room, the aim of the game being to throw rubber hooks at a board with numbers painted on it, and see who could get the highest score.

'Quoits' was another game we used to play. A hole was cut in one of the seats in the taproom and we had to stand on the opposite side of the room and throw the quoits, which were like rubber heels, into the hole. Some nights the competition grew very fierce, with everyone standing round and shouting encouragement to the contestants.

One of the most popular games was 'Bull Ringles' and the old boys often used to challenge each other to a game, the loser having to buy the winner a couple of pints of beer at the end. To play 'Bull Ringles' a ring which had a line about four feet long hanging from it, was screwed into the ceiling of the taproom. Another ring was attached to the end of the line which you had to toss up on to a hook in the wall, close to the ceiling. A good player could score perhaps nineteen or twenty times out of twenty and we usually played twenty or fifty up.

'Spinners' was another game played on the ceiling of the taproom — fortunately the ceilings in all the pubs in Welney were very low in those days, so no one had difficulty in reaching them. The spinners were like large clock-hands screwed into the ceiling with numbers painted round them. We spun the hands round and the one who scored the most points won a pint of beer.

The most popular game at the Three Tuns was, without doubt, darts. Georgie and I became very good at the game, although when we first started to play the landlady's son used to get all his beer money out of us. He would approach us when we went into the pub and say, 'Come on, I'll play you for a couple of pints!' He usually allowed us to win the first two games before starting to play properly and he always managed to come out top in the end. After a lot of practice I won the darts cup in the village one year, and was the runner-up another year. The cup was donated by Elgood's, the local brewery.

During wartime we had a very good darts' team in the village. We visited Wisbech, Ely and Downham Market to play in darts' matches and held regular tournaments in Welney where we collected money to provide comfort for our troops who were fighting overseas. Sometimes the local butcher gave us a joint of beef for a prize at a home match, and that was always keenly contested because food was so short during the war.

4

Ferryman

When I was a boy my father operated the ferry across the washes when the road from Welney Bridge to Suspension Bridge was under water. Flooding occurred during most winters and sometimes the road was impassable for as long as twelve weeks at a time, and everyone had to rely on my father to ferry them across. In recent years, since the building of the new sluices at Earith and Wellmore, the water disappears more quickly and the road is never flooded for more than a week or two.

As soon as I was old enough I was expected to help my father row his passengers about three-quarters of a mile across the flooded washes. We started at seven o'clock in the morning and the postman was always our first customer, followed by men who worked on the farms at the other side of the washes. At nine o'clock our last regular passenger of the morning, Miss Curtiss, the teacher at Suspension Bridge school, had to be ferried to work. For the remainder of the day people often trying to cycle from Wisbech to Ely, would knock on the door of our house and ask to be taken across the washes. At twelve o'clock we had to go over to Suspension Bridge to pick up the postman; at four o'clock the teacher, and then the farm labourers. After tea we had to start again because there were people wanting to go to the cinema in Littleport, or young men wanting to go courting the girls who lived on the other side of the washes.

In those days there were no telephones in Welney and any urgent messages had to be transmitted by telegraph for the postman to deliver. Sometimes the postman called us out in the middle of the night, if he had an important telegram to deliver on the other side of the Washes. I remember one pitch-dark night in the middle of winter when we were awoken by the postman hammering on our door. Father hung his head out of the window to see who it was and, when he realised it was the postman, he hurried downstairs to let him in. Then he called up the stairs to me to tell me to get up. I clambered out of bed, shivering and half asleep, put on some clothes and was soon in the boat with my father and the postman. When we reached the other side the postman still had another two miles to walk to reach the cottage where he had to deliver his telegram, so father and I went to The Crown to wait until he returned. We were always sure of a warm welcome there whatever the hour, and we sat round the fire with Mrs Malkin, the landlady, drinking and exchanging some local gossip. Whilst the postman was away the wind got up and when he eventually reappeared it was blowing a gale outside, so we decided to wait a little longer to see if the wind would abate, because the stretch of water we had to cross was very rough and very high. After a while my father and the postman agreed to risk the return journey, so we left the cosy warmth of the pub and set off for home. The boat rocked from side to side as we were buffeted by the wind and drenched by the waves. When we were about a quarter of the way across the washes we ran into a tree in the darkness. The boat immediately started to fill up with water and we soon lost all sense of direction. Instead of heading for home we went straight down the wash in the opposite direction, got shipwrecked and ended up on the same side as we had started out from, but about a mile further up the bank. By this time it was so dark that we realised that we would never find our home that night, so we made our way back to the pub and knocked up the old landlady who by this time had retired to bed. She let us in and very kindly gave us something to eat before handing us a candle to light our way upstairs to bed. My father, carrying the candle, led the way up the narrow staircase followed by the postman with me close on their heels.

Suddenly, near the top of the stairs, my father faltered, missed the step, slipped and fell backwards, knocking over the postman who in turn knocked me flying. We all landed in a heap at the bottom of the stairs, but fortunately father had managed to hang on to the candle, which was still burning brightly. Eventually we managed to sort ourselves out, and slowly and carefully we mounted the stairs again and got safely into bed. Next morning we awoke to bright sunshine and the water was as calm as a mill pond; we rescued the boat, baled it out and returned home to where my mother and the postman's mother were consoling each other, thinking that we had all been drowned in the night. During the storm when we had all been floundering about in the boat, the postman had lost his glasses, so as soon as we arrived home he had to go off to Wisbech to buy a new pair because he could not see a thing without them. After he'd gone father sent me outside to clean up the boat, where I soon found his glasses wedged under the floor boards.

When the water was on the road one of our regular jobs was to take the beer in a dray to The Crown at Suspension Bridge. It was brewed by Ogden and Phillips in March and, in return for ferrying their beer to The Crown, the brewery allowed us one gallon of beer in bottles in addition to a cash payment. Often we carried the beer over in the mornings at the same time as the workmen, stacking it on board before they arrived. One morning when the workmen had climbed into the boat and sat down alongside the beer, my father and I set off to row to Suspension Bridge. We had our backs to our passengers and it was fairly dark. Unbeknown to us, they started helping themselves to beer, drinking it and throwing the empty bottles over the side and into the water. When we arrived at the The Crown that day Mrs Malkin checked our delivery as usual and was very put out when she discovered that some of the beer was missing. She immediately turned on my father and I and accused us of being responsible. Naturally we denied all knowledge of the missing beer and in fact were very

We all landed in a heap at the bottom of the stairs

indignant that she should suspect us. In spite of all we said we could not convince Mrs Malkin that we knew nothing about it. Later the workmen heard that we were being blamed for taking the missing beer and in trouble with the landlady; they all went to the pub and confessed to her they they they had taken the beer for a joke. She didn't think that it was very funny, but was quick to apologise to us for placing the blame at our door.

One day my father had to ferry old Will Kent, the shepherd, from Suspension Bridge to the pub in Welney because the road was under three feet of water. On the way over he and my father started to argue about something; I don't know exactly what it was, but by the end of the journey Will was in such a rage with my father that he shouted at him, 'Don't bother to take me back, I'll walk!' He was as good as his word and, when he had finished drinking in Welney, he walked all the way to Suspension Bridge, wading through water up to his waist. When he reached the other side he went squelching into The Crown, emptied the water out of his pockets all over the taproom floor and sat down by the fire to dry off, steam rising up all around him. Mrs Malkin was furious with him for bringing all that water into the pub and spilling it over the floor, and she told him in very plain language to 'Clear off'. Will, as usual, was quite unrepentant and took not the slightest bit of notice of her.

Ernie Moxon, a navvy who worked on the farms around Welney, was another regular passenger. Like many old Fenmen he was a hard drinker, and it was not unusual for him to be drunk for a week at a time. One day we had to bring him back to Welney after he'd spent several hours drinking at The Crown. Our only other passenger on that trip was the parson. Ernie climbed unsteadily into the boat, helped by my father and I. Once he was safely aboard he attempted to sit down without assistance, but he was so unstable on his legs that instead of sitting he fell over the seat backwards with his legs in the boat and his body hanging over the side, his head partially submerged

The parson watched with fascination as Ernie Moxon
floundered in the water

in the water. The parson watched with fascination as Ernie, with his hat still on his head, floundered about in the water, and he thought that it was so funny that he laughed until his body shook. After a few moments Ernie looked at him and shouted, 'You'd let any bugger drown afor you'd pull him out.' Still the parson continued to laugh, quite helpless, tears streaming down his cheeks. He was quite incapable of assisting as father and I hauled Ernie back into the boat. Poor old Ernie! He sat down, a sorry sight, as water dripped off him in a steady steam and formed a large pool at his feet. No one said a word at first; the parson tried hard to contain his laughter, and Ernie sat there, glaring. Suddenly, he burst out laughing, the tension disappeared and the rest of us joined in until the old boat began to rock from side to side and there was a danger that someone else might go overboard.

When Ernie went on a drinking spree he would leave home at the usual time each morning with his dinner bag on his back and pretend that he was going to work. His dinner bag was actually a small corn sack with a draw string top in which he carried his bread and cheese. He was well known at all the pubs in the area and they opened their doors early to let him in; he would stay there all day sitting in a corner, drinking pint after pint of beer. Fortunately he had no wife or children to support; he lived with his mother and his sister in a tiny cottage on the Old Bedford Bank, not far from Welney Bridge. One night he staggered out of the pub and walked along the bank to his cottage, plaiting his legs as he went. When he arrived home he saw that his mother had left some kindling, which she had gathered that afternoon, stacked in the hearth, ready to light the fire when she got up the following morning. He managed to pick it up, put it in the grate and light the fire; then he put some sausages in the frying pan and started to cook them. He was making so much noise, stumbling about and crashing into the furniture, that his mother and his sister came down the stairs in their nightdresses to see what all the commotion was about. They struggled with him, trying to get the frying pan out of his hands, and he retaliated by picking up a pound of butter from the table and throwing it at them. It missed, but hit the door leading to the staircase where it stuck to the lock. Poor Mrs Moxon and her daughter had a dreadful time trying to calm Ernie down and coax him to bed before they could start to clear up all the mess.

In wintertime my father was never keen on getting out of his warm bed when anyone knocked him up in the middle of the night and asked to be taken across the washes. The only exception was when the postman called, because he knew that his reason for going across would be genuinely urgent. More often than not my father sent anybody else who came to Joey Butcher who helped him with the ferry when he was very busy. One night when it was very late, around midnight I think, a man came hammering at our door. Father got out of bed, flung open the window and called down, 'Who is it, what do you want?'

The man shouted up, 'I need to go across to Suspension Bridge very urgently, please could you take me straight away?'

'Well,' father drawled, 'I don't rightly know, you'll have to go and ask Joey Butcher; he lives next door, just along the bankside here.'

The man disappeared and went along to Joey's house and knocked him up.

'I have to go across to Suspension Bridge straight away,' he told Joey.

'What, at this time of night!' Joey exclaimed.

'Yes, it's very important. I'll pay you anything you like if you'll take me across now.'

After hearing that there was no more hesitation on Joey's part. He quickly put on his clothes, led his passenger down to the boat and started to row across the washes. The water was not very high that night and every so often little patches of dry land appeared, sticking out above the level of the water. Joey said nothing as he rowed, and the only sound was the slapping of the oars as they hit the water. Suddenly when they were about half way across the water, the man spoke up and said, 'Well, old mate, I'm sorry; I haven't any money so I won't be able to pay you after all.'

Still Joey said nothing; he just carried on rowing. A few moments later they reached one of the little islands and Joey turned to the man and said casually, 'Hop out a minute mate, I shall have to scup up, water is getting into the bottom of the boat.'

The man jumped out straight away and landed on the tiny patch of dry land and Joey, quick as a flash, pushed off again shouting, 'You can stay there 'til the morning. You can't pay so I'm taking you no further.' And sure enough he left the man to spend the rest of the night there until somebody rowed over again in daylight and rescued him.

When I was sixteen my father handed the ferry over to me. I took complete charge of it and ran it with just a little help from my father at times. I continued to run it all through World War II and was sometimes asked to carry soldiers from one side of the washes to the other when they were in the area on manœuvres. I finally had to retire from the job in 1950 when I suffered a bad attack of rheumatic fever. For our family it was the end of an era, because we had run that ferry for over a hundred years. No one took it over after I finished because by then people no longer relied on it as much as they did when I was a youngster. The wash road had been raised by about a foot which meant that cars could get through more often when it was flooded, and people could even wade through in wellington boots when the water was not too high. Drainage in the washes has improved so much now that the road is rarely flooded for more than a week at a time, and people wanting to go to Ely by car can take a detour round by Downham Market.

5
Will Kent

When I was a youngster the most influential person in my life was, without doubt, Will Kent, the shepherd who lived out in the washes. I suppose he must have been about fifty when I first knew him; a man of medium height and build, with a thatch of grey hair and a moustache. He was a friend of my father's and, like him, was an eel-catcher and punt-gunner. He lived way out in the washes and very few people were encouraged to visit him.

I remember clearly the first time I went to his house; I was only a small boy at the time, and was asked by Will to take some ducks to his house for him. I happened to be at home one day when Will called to buy some decoy ducks from my father. The punt-gunners all used these decoy ducks; they put the decoys into pens out in the washes to attract and call down the wild ducks so that they could shoot them. Will paid my father for the birds, turned to me, and holding out his hand said, 'Here's sixpence for you if you'll carry these ducks in a sack to my house for me.'

Always glad to earn some extra money, I took the sack and the sixpence and after receiving directions, set off. His house turned out to be three miles away, right in the middle of the washes about two miles from Suspension Bridge. It was completely isolated, his only neighbours being the birds; there were hundreds of them all around his house. No one ever interfered with Will; he was king of his small domain.

The room where the family lived was dominated by the fireplace which was flanked at each side by a cupboard. Standing in the centre of the room was an old, square table which was always covered by a dark-green fringed cloth. The only other items of furniture in that room were two windsor chairs, one for Will and one for Mrs Kent, two kitchen chairs for their children Polly and Ernie, a horse-hair sofa which prickled the backs of your legs when you sat on it and a chest of drawers. Hanging on the wall was a big, old square clock, Will's pride and joy, which he wound up each night without fail. The floor was covered with peg rugs that Mrs Kent made herself from scraps of material which she cut up from old clothes. In the other downstairs room were two spare kitchen chairs, another chest of drawers and a harmonium that no one in the family could play. During the shooting season this room was usually packed full of birds which Will had shot.

On that first visit to Will's home, Mrs Kent made me very welcome. She was a nice old girl. If I close my eyes I can see her now, standing in the doorway of their cottage, her dark hair streaked with grey. She invited me in that day for a cup of tea, the first of many I was to share with her over the years as we sat chatting beside the well-stoked fire. We talked about all kinds of things on our first meeting and the time flew by very quickly. When I got up to go Mrs Kent said to me, 'You're welcome to come and visit us at any time,' adding the warning, 'but if you tell them up in Welney what we do here, you'll never come again.' I was to hear those words repeated many times in the future: they made sure I understood that I could see all but say nothing!

Sometimes the old house was full of the birds Will had shot. We packed them up into sacks, about a hundred in each sack and I took them to Littleport Station for him, carrying them on my handlebars and the back of my bike. It was a distance of about six miles, but I was young then and nothing seemed too heavy or too much for me. The birds were loaded onto the London train and then de-spatched to Leadenhall Market.

In wintertime it is very bleak out in the washes, especially when it is wet or foggy. The Delph and the

Hundred Foot bound an area which consists of mile after mile of flat land, whose surface is only occasionally interrupted by the odd clump of trees. In the middle of all this wilderness lived the Kent family. Everything they needed had to be brought over the Hundred Foot river by boat. The butcher, baker and grocer came from Littleport once a week to deliver goods to the farm cottages located on the other side of the river from the Kents. When they had been to the cottages the delivery men used to stand on the opposite bank and either shout to Mrs Kent or blow a whistle to let her know they were there. When she heard them she got into the boat and punted across the river, her long skirt billowing out behind, to collect whatever she needed for the following week. In spite of the difficulties of obtaining provisions, there was always plenty to eat and drink in that house. Will raised his own pigs, cows and chickens and always kept a good stock of beer in. Mrs Kent was a wonderful cook. She made all her own bread and cakes in the oven beside the fire and her Yorkshire puddings were the best I have ever tasted.

The washes flooded every winter and when the water rose above three feet on the road we knew that Will's house would be flooded. When this happened, the Kents moved all their belongings upstairs and then left the house to stay at one of the various pubs in the area, or with Jarman Smart and his wife who lived in the cottage I live in now. They were very friendly with the Smarts because Mrs Smart used to knit all Will's plover nets for him. I used to accompany Will regularly when he went back to check on the house during the floods. He did this every day because he had to go back to feed the livestock which he always moved, along with the hen coops, on to the top of the bank where it was dry. One day, wearing long thigh boots, we went to look over the house as usual and for some reason which I have now forgotten, we decided to go inside; to our surprise, we found a bottle of whisky floating about in the living room. Will, always ready with an excuse for a drink, managed to rescue it and he opened it up and shared it with me, saying, 'A good drink of this will soon warm us up, bor!'

When the flooding reached its height, Will cut marks on the door frame to show where the water had been and until last year, although only part of the house remained, those marks could still be seen. Now, alas, the rest of the house has just been demolished by the Royal Society for the Protection of Birds, who own the wash in which it stood. When the water went down Mrs Kent would return to the cottage and give it a good clean. It always surprised me how quickly the old house dried out, and after a couple of days there was never any smell to remind us of the flooding. Even more amazing was the fact that, although flooding occurred every winter, it never seemed to worry the Kents. They just accepted it as a regular part of their lives and I never heard either of them grumble about it or express a wish to live elsewhere.

I used to look forward to Saturdays when I could spend the day at the Kent's cottage, and I helped with all kinds of jobs: feeding the ducks and chickens, milking the cows, digging worms to feed the decoy birds, or exercising the greyhounds. Will always kept greyhounds; they were his other hobby besides drinking! I used to exercise them in the washes where there were plenty of hares for them to chase. Very often they caught the hares and provided Mrs Kent with the ingredients for some very tasty meals.

I remember Will once owning a very fine pony. He was really proud of it and although someone once offered him quite a large sum of money for it, he refused to sell it. Not long after he'd received this offer we were out in the washes exercising the dogs, when one of them cut loose and started to chase the pony. No amount of calling and shouting on Will's part could bring the dog to heel; it was having a great time chasing the pony wherever it went, barking at its heels in excitement. The poor old pony became more and more nervous and agitated, racing wildly in one direction and then in another in its efforts to escape from the dog. Eventually, Will managed to catch the dog and bring it to heel. He then went after the pony, only to discover, as he was stroking it to try and calm it down, that during the course of the chase it had somehow dislocated its shoulder. Mrs Kent was absolutely furious when she heard about it, and she turned on Will angrily and shouted, 'You should've sold that pony when you had the chance. You'll never sell it now, who'd want a pony with a dislocated shoulder. You can say goodbye to that money you could've got for him.' Will glared at her, hands on his hips. 'I'll show you,' he retorted. And he did, because on the following Sunday morning he gathered together some of the men who worked on the nearby farms and, watched by his wife, he carefully put two ropes round the pony's head like a halter. With the help of the farm labourers he then pulled the pony into the Hundred Foot river, knowing that the animal would instinctively strike out and start to swim, which it did. This action caused the shoulder to 'click' back into position again, much to Will's relief. Mrs Kent never mentioned it again!

Whenever Will went on a drinking spree, which was quite often, I tried to spend more time than usual at the cottage, so that I could keep an eye on things for Mrs Kent and help her with the extra jobs which came up through Will's absence. Usually his bouts of drinking would last for about a fortnight, and during that time he would be waiting outside the pub at Suspension Bridge when it opened at half past ten in the morning and would stay there drinking all day, only returning home when it closed at ten o'clock at night. Normally he had to borrow a lamp from someone in the pub to light his way home. They all used old candle-lanterns in those days and Will went staggering off down the bank with the lantern bobbing to and fro as he held it unsteadily in his hand. The following morning he could never remember who he had borrowed the lantern from, so he never bothered to return it; there was always a large collection of candle lanterns sitting on the shelves in his shed. Sometimes I would find one in the middle of the bank halfway to his house, because he often stopped on his way home, put the lantern down and then forgot all about it when he went on his way again.

Each spring I helped Mrs Kent to sweep the chimney. She used to go to the straw stack and pull a good sized bunch of straw out of a bale, and then tie the straw to the middle of a cart rope which had a light weight on the end. I had to climb up on to the roof with the rope and drop it down the chimney to the old lady who was waiting at the bottom to catch the weight. Together we then proceeded to see-saw the rope up and down the chimney, the bunch of straw sweeping the soot down. One day I climbed up on to the roof and threw the rope down just as Mrs Kent poked her head up the chimney to say something to me. The weight hit her smack on the head and made her eyes water. She was furious! I sat there on the roof, safely out of her way, whilst she ranted and raged at me and called me some fine old names.

Most of the time Will never worried about anyone or anything. The only creatures he could not stand were rats, which for some reason, terrified him. Inside his cottage there was a large, heavy curtain which hung between the two downstairs rooms to keep out the draughts. One winter's night I was sitting round the kitchen table with the family, having my supper by the light of an old oil-lamp which was hanging over the table. We were all chatting quite happily together when suddenly I saw a rat in the shadows, peeping round the corner of the curtain. Will saw it too and drew back in his chair, a look of pure horror on his face. I jumped up, grabbed the poker and tried to hit the rat with it, but it was too quick for me; it shot behind the curtain and disappeared. Now the family had known for some weeks that this rat was about because it had been eating Polly Kent's silk stockings, but this was the first time any of them had actually seen it. Will's son and I decided that we would search right through the house that night until we found it, so we lit another couple of lanterns and started to pull out the furniture and peer underneath it. We looked inside cupboards, behind curtains and under

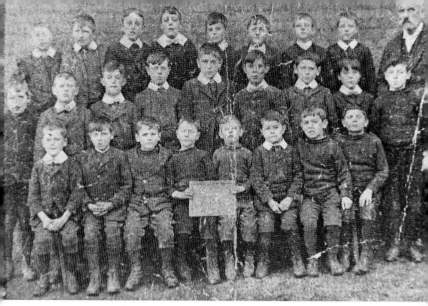

Welney Old School boys: Ernie is in the front row on the extreme right, with the dreaded Mr Bearcock behind

Ernie (with the oars) and Alfred James (standing) taking passengers across the washes to Suspension Bridge

Alf and Ernie ferrying the postman to Suspension Bridge

Will Kent's old house

Comparing punt guns

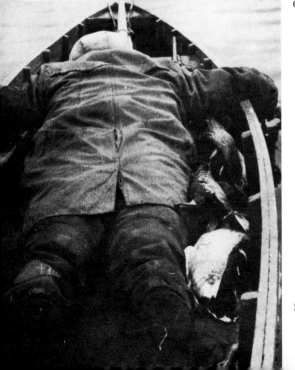

Stalking the ducks

Firing the punt gun

(*below*) Returning home from punt-gunning; (*bottom*) The willow beds and flooded washes

Setting the plover nets

Netting plovers

Stripping the willow

Weaving a grig

(*left*) Repairing an eel-net; (*right*) Setting eel-traps in Old Bedford river

Resetting an eel-net in the river Delph

Drying the eel-nets in the
'rod-peeling place'

Ernie still sharpens his
skates each winter

beds but there was no sign of the rat anywhere. Finally, we dragged out the old harmonium which stood in the front room and, when we looked inside, it was all chambled. The rat had obviously been living there for some time, quite undisturbed because no one in the family ever played the instrument. Will's son Ernie had bought it years ago at an auction sale in the village, because the girl he courted had played it in the chapel on Sundays. He courted that girl for twenty years before he found the courage to propose to her. When he did, she accepted and they were eventually married. The harmonium meanwhile had remained in the Kent's front room and provided a cosy home for the rat. I picked up the lantern and, holding it aloft, peered closely inside the harmonium. I could see the rat looking up at me from its nest, so I got Ernie to pass me a stick and I managed to kill it. Will had not taken part in the hunt for the rat, but he heaved a great sigh of relief as I carried it from the house and threw it on the bank.

When Will was a young lad he lived with his parents and brother Henry on the high bank between the Delph and the Old Bedford, close to the railway lines. His family lived like hermits and were all more or less wild, although old Mr Kent was very strict with the boys and they knew that they would soon get a good thrashing if they upset him. One day Will and Henry got up to some mischief; I don't know exactly what it was, but they knew that their father would be really angry when he discovered what they had been up to. It must have been bad because they were both convinced that he would kill them when he caught them, so they hid in a fish trunk for a week, only coming out when they were sure that their father was not around. They had no food and so lived on cracks. (Cracks are also called bullies or bulloses and they grew in abundance round Welney in those days. People used to gather them to make jam.) Eventually hunger drove them back home and much to their relief, all was forgiven.

One day the two boys started fighting over something, and Will hit Henry over the head with a willow, cutting right through the top of his ear. Will was reminded of that fight every time he looked at his brother because until the day he died poor Henry only had half an ear on one side with a flap of loose skin hanging from it. If the injury had occurred today, the ear would have been stitched back together again, but in those days no one ever thought of going to the doctor with anything like that.

Sometimes I walk down the bank now and look across the washes to where Will's house once stood, and I remember all the happy hours I spent there and all the things he taught me. His kind of life is gone forever: it will never return. Although his existence was often very hard, he enjoyed it and would not have changed places with any man. He could neither read nor write: I don't think he ever went to school. He never travelled far from Welney, but his life was rich in experience because he lived so close to nature and appreciated all aspects of it. He knew every inch of the washes and all the birds and creatures who made their homes there, because his livelihood depended upon this knowledge.

6
Punt-gunners and Wildfowling

The father of all punt-gunners was Hagan Smart, the shepherd who lived in a cottage with the unusual name of 'Norway House'. His father, in his young days, had been a very good ice skater, and after winning the National Championship in 1890, he went over to Norway to skate. He earned enough money there to build a new house on his return, which he called 'Norway House'.

Sometimes even now when I stand in the middle of the washes, Hagan's old hunting ground, I can picture him quite clearly flat in his long punt, hands hanging over the sides, gently propelling the boat through the water, stalking the birds. During the summer months Hagan looked after about five hundred acres of washes and several hundred head of cattle which grazed on them. He checked the animals twice a day, making sure that none had fallen into the dykes. Sometimes after a thunderstorm he'd find six or seven bullocks trapped in the dykes where they'd sought shelter from the storm and he had to get help to haul them out with blocks and pulleys. The rest of the time was spent cleaning out ditches and making sure that everything was ready for the wildfowl which he knew would return for the winter. He was always thinking about ducks; he was always talking about ducks; he claimed that he always dreamt about ducks! He was certainly always planning how he was going to hunt them when the shooting season came round again.

Hagan was a wonderful shot with the puntgun. When he was out on those washes stalking the birds he was very patient and never hurried, but silently crept up on the ducks until he had them within his sights. Even when he was within firing distance he did not always discharge his gun. If he thought that the ducks were not sitting right for him to get what he considered to be a good shot, he would just go away and leave them without attempting to fire his gun. Sometimes when I saw him do this I said, 'You could have shot at least a dozen there.' 'Don't you worry, Ernie,' he would reply, 'there'll be another day and I'll try them again.' I have seen him spend hours stalking the birds and then watching and waiting until he had them all within the stroke of a shot before he fired and consequently he rarely made a bad shot.

His father, Jim Fish Smart, and his grandfather before him were punt-gunners and he was only a young lad when he started. He once described to me how his father turned to him one day and said, 'There's a pair of ducks out there, you can go and have a shot at them.'

Old Jim Fish went and got his big punt gun which he called 'The Old Lion', primed it for Hagan and put it into the boat. Now Hagan, who had never shot before, was afraid of that big gun, but he dared not admit it to his father; when he got within firing range of the ducks, he started knocking the stalking sticks against the side of the boat in the hope that the noise would frighten the birds and they would fly away, but without success. The ducks continued sitting there, a perfect target. Suddenly his father who was standing on the bank watching shouted, 'You're close enough, let go!'

Hagan, shocked into action, pulled the trigger and, much to his surprise, killed both ducks. With the firing of that first shot he made an important discovery; he had no reason to fear the gun anymore, since it did him no harm. His father allowed him to shoot several times again that season and he really began to enjoy it. As he grew older he developed into a very good shot and became as cunning as a fox and as wary as any bird that flew. He always knew where the birds would be at first light in the morning, because he used to put corn down the night before to attract them. Many of the birds came in from the coast to feed at first light before going back again, so he had to be up very early to catch them.

When I was a lad there were six or seven other professional wildfowlers about here. There was immense rivalry between them and they all had their own stretch of wash, measuring about a mile, which they jealously guarded. Starting at the bottom end of the washes, Hagan Smart's territory was near Salter's Lode; Cutty See, Will Smart, Joey Butcher and the two Kent brothers, Harry and Will all had their own patches between there and Welney. They never strayed on to each other's piece of land unless by accident when it was foggy.

Will Kent was my tutor when I first started punt-gunning, and he was very strict with me. Before he would allow me to go with him into the washes on a shooting expedition I had to learn how to prepare his big gun and clean it out after he had used it. I had a long rod with a worm on the end — a worm being a piece of iron shaped like a corkscrew which was made by the local blacksmith. I wound a piece of rag around the worm, dipped it in water and pushed it up and down inside the barrel to clean it. I then replaced the wet rag with a piece of dry cloth and dried out the barrel. Next I poured gunpowder into the measure which was placed in the muzzle of the gun, and tipped the gun up so that the powder ran down the barrel and into the breach. Next I made a wad with hay or tissue paper and rammed that down the barrel with the gun rod until it was pressed tight against the powder, and then poured the same amount of lead shot into the measure and tipped that down the barrel in the same way. I made another lighter wad, put that on top of the shot and rammed it down as tightly as I could. My next job was to wipe the pan dry and put a feather in the touch hole. I put a piece of rag on top of the feather and then let the hammer down on top of the rag to keep the pan dry. Finally I covered the gun down in the punt, until it was required.

It was only when Will was satisfied that I knew how to clean and prepare the gun properly that he allowed me to go out into the washes with him one morning to stalk some ducks. It was a bright, sunny day and everything looked beautiful; the blue sky overhead and the water shimmering like diamonds in the light of the reflected sun. I lay down flat in the boat behind the gun, just as I had watched Will do so many times, and taking up the stalking-sticks, one in each hand and holding them over the side of the boat, I propelled myself steadily along the wash to where I could see about a dozen birds feeding in the water. I stopped about seventy or eighty yards away from them, took aim, pulled the trigger and fired the gun. I only managed to kill three ducks that first time. The others flew off, quickly disappearing into the distance. Although most of the birds escaped, I was very pleased with that first attempt. I gathered up the dead ducks, threw them into the back of the punt and returned to Will's cottage feeling very proud of myself. Mrs Kent saw me approaching out of the window and came out to meet me. 'Well done, my old bor,' she said, patting me on the back as I held up my three trophies to show her.

After that I was often allowed to borrow Will's gun, but only if there was no one else around. 'You'd never shoot yourself,' Will used to say, 'but you might easily shoot someone else.' Whenever I returned to the cottage feeling dejected because I had nothing in my bag after a day's shooting, Mrs Kent would be there to cheer me up and offer a few words of encouragement. 'Never mind, there's another day, you'll do better next time.'

I bagged more and more ducks as I improved with practice. After a year or two my father bought me my own punt-gun from his friend Joey Butcher, and when I was about eighteen I started out as a professional wildfowler. During the shooting season which lasted from 1 September to 31 January I went out every morning at first light when the washes were flooded. They always looked beautiful early in the morning with the newly risen sun shining on the water. Sometimes there were curtains of ducks, widgeons and teals wheeling about in the sky, almost blotting out the sun. After I'd had a shot, I went home for breakfast and then went out again, taking my lunch with me. I often stayed out all day in all weathers. The colder, frostier or snowier it was, the more ducks I shot; sometimes as many as twenty ducks before breakfast. When my wife saw them she would say, 'You've had a good bag this morning then!' If, however, I went out and shot nothing she grumbled, 'You might just as well have laid abed.'

Early morning was always the best time for shooting ducks. Often I went out before it was light and lay in the bottom of my punt within sixty yards of the ducks. I could not see them, only hear them, splashing about in the water, washing themselves, getting ready to go back to the coast. I positioned my boat to the west of the birds so that when daylight broke I could see them in the first glimmer of light from the east. After a few minutes it was light enough to get a shot. I have killed hundreds of ducks at that time of the morning. It was also easier in the morning to pick up the crippled birds, the ones who were not killed outright, because I was able to see them. When I shot at dusk, it was often too dark to spot them.

The washes did not always flood naturally during the shooting season, and sometimes I had to divert water from the Hundred Foot, the tidal river, into a wash where I wanted to shoot. When I had done this I constructed a battery — a wall of reeds about twenty or thirty feet long and two or three feet high about two or three yards away from the edge of the water. I set my gun up in daylight, resting it on a tressle behind the battery and pointing it through the reeds towards the water, because I always shot into the water. Next I laid a trail of corn leading from the battery to the water where I had penned my decoy ducks. My preparations complete, I went home. I returned at night-time, crawling slowly and quietly on my stomach towards the battery, and after I had primed my gun I lay there motionless in the moonlight, waiting for the ducks. I was always certain they would come, attracted by my decoys and the prospect of food. As protection against the bitter cold of those nights I wore a heavy blue jersey, furlined flying jacket, thick socks and thigh boots, and managed to keep fairly warm. I loved the solitude of the nights spent out there and felt completely at peace, forgetting my own worries and the problems of the rest of the world as I waited patiently for the birds to come and feed on the corn. If the washes were frozen, I cut a hole about twenty yards long in the ice in front of my gun, threw corn into the hole and placed my decoys at the side. If it was snowy, I made sure that the battery was well covered with snow and I wore a white coat as camouflage, so that the ducks would not spot me.

As soon as I had several ducks within the sight of the gun I fired, sometimes killing half a dozen and at other times twenty or thirty. I gathered them up as quickly as I could, threw them in a heap behind the battery and primed my gun up again, ready for the next shot. If there was snow on the ground it was often stained bright red with the blood of the birds I had shot.

This method of shooting the birds was much easier than stalking them on open waters in a punt because the gun resting on the tressle was stable and not affected by any movement. All you had to do was sit and wait.

At the end of a day's or night's shooting I took the ducks home and hung them in their feathers from the beams in the dairy. When there were fifty or a hundred suspended from the ceiling I packed them into bags, rode into Ely with them on my bicycle and loaded them on to the passenger train for London, where they were sold at Leadenhall Market. At Christmastime we used to let the ducks hang in the dairy for a week or two; there were so many turkeys and geese about that not many people wanted to buy wildfowl, and the price dropped. So we kept them, not offering them for sale until after the new year when the price started to rise again.

During World War II ducks were making one pound per brace, so if you only managed to kill ten in a day you were doing quite well. I always aimed to shoot mallard rather than widgeon because, being larger, they made twice as much money. Sometimes I killed a few wild geese, usually pink-feet; but they did not make any more money than ducks. In those days I paid about fourpence (old money) per pound for shot and one shilling per pound for powder, and I bought it in two stone bags. When I took a shot I used about twelve ounces of shot (or one pound if I was using my biggest gun) and two ounces of powder to force it out. Today shot is twenty-five pence per pound and powder one pound per pound.

The old punt-gunners, who were all wonderful characters, used to gather in the pubs every night; most of them were hard drinkers and liked nothing better than sharing a good story over a glass of beer. They sat there night after night, boasting to each other about the number of shots they had had and how many birds they had bagged that day. They all exaggerated because there was great rivalry between these old boys, and they each wished to be known as 'the best shot' in the washes. They all knew that the claims they made were wildly extravagant and they often ended up fighting with each other before the night was over.

Shooting matches were held in Welney each year and all the old punt-gunners took part. They were very popular events, which all the locals eagerly looked forward to and were keenly contested by the participants because there was always a good prize for the winner. One year my wife's grandfather won the event and, accompanied by the other contestants, he went to the pub to celebrate his victory and receive his prize, which was a bottle of whisky. After the presentation his friends gathered around him, urging him to open the bottle and pass it round.

'Come on, open it up, let's all have a drink,' they said. He was quite determined to save it, and replied, 'No, I'm not opening it here, I'm taking it home for another day.'

Carefully picking up the bottle he put it into the inside pocket of his jacket, completely forgetting that there was a large hole in it. Naturally the bottle went straight through the hole and crashed on to the floor, breaking into hundreds of tiny pieces. Joey Butcher who was leaning against the wall watching remarked, 'That just serves you right for not sharing it with us; you've lost it now.' As grandfather Smart sadly looked at his whisky spreading across the floor, Joey suddenly got down on his hands and knees. 'I'm not going to waste all that good whisky,' he said; and with that he started to lap it up from the floor just like a dog. How he managed to do it without cutting his tongue on the tiny pieces of glass I'll never know.

Old Will Kent once told me about a gang of punt-gunners who were celebrating in the pub at Welsh's Dam one night. As usual, conversation in the taproom was all about ducks and shooting. During the course of the night talk somehow got round from the wild ducks in the washes, to the tame ducks which the landlord kept on the river outside the pub. One of the gunners boasted that he could easily kill all ten ducks with one shot and tried to bribe the landlord into letting him have a go. At first the landlord refused to consider the deal, but then he took one of the other wildfowlers to one side and persuaded him to draw the shot out of his friend's gun whilst he tried to divert the man's attention. When this was done the landlord turned to the old gunner and said, 'All right, where's your money? I've decided to let you have a shot at my ducks after all.' The man paid up, and after picking up his gun swaggered outside followed by all his mates. He took aim and fired at the ducks, and was astounded when he realised that he had not managed to kill one single duck; all ten were still there, healthy and quite unharmed. The expression of surprise on his face was so comic that everyone laughed, but Will said that he was too drunk to realise how he had been tricked.

Those old punt-gunners were a really wild bunch and always carried a gun into the pub with them, which was propped up against the wall. This led to some wild shooting on occasions when the old boys were full of beer. One summer's evening Joey Butcher came staggering out of The Three Tuns and, glancing across the field behind the pub, saw Tommy Roof sitting on a chair at the back of The Lamb and Flag having his hair cut by George See. One of the other gunners who had come out of the pub with Joey followed his gaze, and seeing Tommy pointed his finger at him and said, 'I bet you daren't shoot at him.' Joey, full of alcoholic self-confidence, said, 'Course I dare.' Picking up his gun, he took aim and fired at Tommy, hitting him straight in the face. Poor old Tommy, with blood pouring from his face and in a state of shock, was rushed to the doctor. One of Tommy's friends who had been in The Lamb and Flag at the time of the shooting called the police,

'I'm not going to waste all that good whisky'

who were quick to arrive and took Joey off to Downham Market gaol where he was locked up in the cells for the night.

Word spread round the village like wildfire and next morning everyone was talking about the shooting, the men gathered in the smithy and the women in the village shop. Tongues wagged all day long, everyone sympathising with Tommy and shaking their heads over Joey. In spite of what had happened, however, Joey was not without friends and some of them pooled their money and went over to Downham Market the following morning and managed to bail him out. Later when he appeared before the magistrate he was very repentant, but the magistrate was not impressed and severely reprimanded Joey before fining him. Again his friends rallied round and paid the fine for him because he had very little money. Surprisingly he and Tommy, who soon recovered, remained the best of friends until they died.

Joey had no malice in his nature and was popular in the village because he was generous towards his friends and ready to have a laugh and joke with anyone he met. His mother, who kept The Eagle Tavern for several years, was taken ill one night and she had to send for Joey to look after the pub whilst she retired to her bed. There was an almost carnival atmosphere in The Eagle that night because the place was crowded, word having quickly got round that 'Joey was in charge'. Drink flowed freely and everyone thoroughly enjoyed themselves. By the end of the evening nearly all the customers were more than a little merry and they staggered home in twos and threes, supporting each other and singing at the tops of their voices. When everyone had gone, Joey, feeling very happy and pleased with himself, closed the bar and went upstairs to see how his mother was faring. He opened the door to her bedroom and poked his head round, a big grin on his face. 'How are you feeling mother?' he asked. 'We've had a really good night downstairs.'

'That's good,' said Mrs Butcher. 'Where are the takings?

You'd better let me have them so that I can put the money away later.'

Joey's face fell a fraction and his voice lost some of its confidence.

'Takings mother?' he asked in an uncertain voice.

'Yes, the money you took from all those people down-stairs tonight,' Mrs Butcher said impatiently.

'Oh, I never bothered to take any money from them,' he said.

'You idiot!' she cried. 'Do you mean to tell me that you let them drink all that beer without charging them for it?'

She tried to get out of bed to hit Joey, but fortunately for him she was too weak. I think that she would have killed him that night had she not been feeling so ill.

Every Friday a travelling salesman by the name of Mr Ladyman came to Welney from March, with his horse and cart, to deliver groceries. He was always accompanied by a boy who had to look after the horse and feed it before they returned to March. When he had delivered all his goods, Mr Ladyman used to go to The Eagle Tavern to quench his thirst and he left his horse stabled by the side of the tavern with the boy in charge of it whilst he enjoyed a beer or two. One day the lad was waiting patiently by the door of the stables when Joey came rolling out of the pub with his gun under his arm, half drunk as usual. The boy, seeing the state Joey was in, began to laugh and said, 'Ha, I bet you can't hit anything with that gun of yours now!'

'Who says?' asked Joey. 'Just throw your hat up in the air and I'll show you.'

The boy, still giggling at Joey, snatched off his hat and tossed it up into the air whilst Joey stood and watched, but made no attempt to shoot at it until it landed on the ground; whereupon he just rested his gun on top of the hat and blasted it to pieces. When the lad saw what had happened to his hat he burst into tears and roared so loudly that Mr Ladyman came dashing out of the pub to see what had happened. When he heard the full story he turned on the boy and said, 'That just serves you right. Let it be a

When the hat landed on the ground Joey blasted it to pieces

lesson to you never to make fun of Joey again.'

By the end of World War II nearly all the old punt-gunners had either retired or died, and there were few men to replace them. Josh Scott, an old friend of mine, had done a little punt-gunning before the war with his father and uncle. They were known locally as dry-land gunners because they did not use a boat, preferring to shoot from a battery instead. After the war, when Josh was demobbed, he acquired his own boat and gun and became a professional wildfowler, as well as giving Hagan Smart an occasional hand when he needed help in his washes. When Hagan fell ill and could not work, he sent for Josh and asked him to take over his washes and shepherd them for him until he was well again. This was in addition to the five hundred acres of land that Josh already shepherded, having inherited them from his father. In return for looking after his washes, Hagan told Josh that he could shoot all over them. Sadly, not long afterwards Hagan died and in his will be bequeathed 'Old Lion', his big punt-gun, to Josh, who continued shepherding and wildfowling until 1968 when the Wildfowl Trust, headed by Sir Peter Scott, took over most of the washes and appointed Josh as warden of the newly established Welney Wildfowl Refuge, a position he held until his retirement in 1983. Josh and I were the last of the professional wildfowlers in these parts.

7

Plover-catching

My old friend Will Kent introduced me to plover-catching. When the cattle went off the washes in September each year, Will used to flood them by diverting the water from the Hundred Foot, the tidal river which runs along side the washes, into wooden tunnels which ran through the banks. These tunnels had doors on the tidal side which could be opened and closed to control the flow of water. In those days no official organisation had any interest in the washes and so there was no one to prevent Will from doing exactly as he liked. Today the washes are owned and controlled by the Royal Society for the Protection of Birds and the Wildfowl Trust, and when they want to flood them for the birds in winter they still use one of Will's old tunnels.

Once the washes were flooded Will put down his plover nets and started to catch the birds. When I was a youngster at school I always looked forward to visiting Will on Saturdays in wintertime because I knew that in all probability he would be out in the washes setting his nets to trap the plovers. It was really exciting for me to watch him at work and I used to hold my breath as I waited for him to toss the net over. I was impatient to help, but I dared not offer my services to Will because this was his territory and it was an unspoken rule that only he could decide what could and could not be done out there: Will's word was law!

I accompanied him week after week in the hope that he would let me help in some way or another, but it was a long time before I was allowed to assist him. I remember how thrilled I was when he finally let me help; I did not care what job he asked me to do just as long as I could be out there with him netting the birds. One Saturday morning I arrived at his house as usual and was met by his wife who told me that I had just missed him: he had gone off to market. She must have realised how disappointed I was by the look on my face because she said, 'Cheer up, bor! Don't worry; Will's left a message saying that you can use his nets today.'

I think back to that day now and still regard it as one of the most memorable I have ever spent. I was out there in the washes, alone except for the wild birds around me; the silence only broken by their calls and the noise of their wings, as I sat there waiting for the plovers to come and land, close to the net. There were millions of them around here in those days.

When a few birds landed on the bed I tensed myself, waiting for the right moment to release the springs on the net and trap the birds. I made many mistakes at first, chiefly through misjudging when to throw the net; but gradually I began to master the art and the number of birds in my bag slowly increased. The end of the day saw me cold, tired, a little wet, but very happy and looking forward to the next Saturday in the hope that Will would let me try my hand again.

Slowly, by careful observation and working alongside Will, I picked up all he knew about plover-catching and a lot more besides. One day after being out in the washes on my own, I returned to to Will's cottage and he asked, 'How many have you caught today then?'

'Two hundred and forty,' I replied.

'That's very good,' he said, I never caught as many as that myself in one day.'

I was successful because I was young then and could nip in and out of the water more quickly than the old men. The nets were always about one hundred and fifty yards away from the hide and it was hard work wading backwards and forwards to them, knee-deep in water.

Sometimes, before the war, I was able to earn a hundred pounds a week from plover-catching, and that was a lot of money in those days. Unlike wildfowling it involved very little expense, because I made my own plover nets, which had three-inch meshes and were twenty yards long by four yards wide. At each end of the net were pulleys with springs attached to them. The springs, which were always under water, were just long poles with toes which went into the ground. They were fastened down with catch-pegs — pieces of wood with a notch on to which the springs were hooked. Attached to the springs was a long line which stretched perhaps one hundred and fifty yards to wherever I was hiding, usually in a purpose-built hut. I had to buy new pulley lines each year, but they never cost me more than five pounds a year.

I set my net anywhere I thought there was likely to be water. Before the water came on to the washes I made a small raft from a wooden frame with wire mesh stretched across it, which was covered with grass. It looked just like a lawn, measuring about twenty yards long and two yards wide, surrounded by water. I had to mow barrow loads of grass to sprinkle on the top of it. The raft was pegged into position so that it would not move and the top of it, hopefully, was just level with the water. The net had to be wider than the raft so that some of it was anchored down by the weight of the water. When the springs were released the net flew over and folded the birds inside, just like a book closing up. If the net was not wide enough, it just turned inside out.

After setting the net I used to sit in my hide watching and waiting. I called the birds down with the aid of decoys which I put on hassocks at the side of the main bed or I whistled them in. The plovers flew over, always against the wind, and dropped down on the bed. I used to love sitting there, just as the sun broke through after a frosty night and watch the birds flying in from the potato fields, their feet covered in mud. They would settle on the water and start to wash themselves, and I could see all the colours of the rainbow reflected on the water as they splashed around. Gradually they came nearer and alighted on the bed, and when there were about twenty or thirty plovers sitting there I would quickly nip the net over them. Wearing big thigh boots, I had to wade in about a foot of water from my hide to where the plovers, with their wings flapping, were trapped by their heads in the meshes of the net. I walked along the net, killing the birds by putting my fingers in the back of their necks. On reaching the end of the net I retraced my steps and pulled the birds through the net, tossing them into the water before resetting it. After gathering up all the dead birds I returned to my hide and resumed the vigil.

I remember Will Kent came with me to set the net one morning just as it was getting light. Although he was an old man then, he ran up and down the side of the raft from one end to the other setting the springs. Suddenly I called out, 'Cor! There are hundreds of birds up there — look at them flying overhead.' Will, anxious to get the net set so that we could start catching the birds, chanced only a quick look up into the sky. As he did so he trod on one of the springs; the net immediately flew over him and hit him on the back of the head. 'Ouch,' he cried, 'More haste, less bloody speed!'

Sometimes I sat out there all day and did not catch a single plover, but at other times I caught ten or twelve pounds worth. At the end of a good day I could hardly see the grass because it had been flattened by all the birds landing on it, and I had to mow another two or three sackfulls to sprinkle on the bed ready for the next morning. I also had to make sure that it was damp, because the birds would never land on a dry bed.

When I had finished for the day I carried all the birds home in sacks and laid them out in the dairy to dry. I smoothed out the feathers, stroked down the wings and twisted the legs up so they were out of sight. The following morning they had dried out and looked presentable; plump and clean with all their feathers nice and smooth, they were ready for sale. I carefully packed them into sacks — usually a hundred and twenty birds in each sack — and took them to

Littleport Station to be loaded onto the passenger train to London, where they were sold in Leadenhall Market. This was often the worst part of the job. It was hard work riding a bike and balancing a sack containing over a hundred birds on the handlebars, especially after a hard day's work in the washes. The six miles from Welney to Littleport seemed more like sixty some nights. Later I got a motor bike which made the journey much easier.

Although I had several contacts in Leadenhall Market I dealt mainly with just three agents. It was important to have more than one outlet for the birds because there were about ten other plover-catchers in the area, and if we all had a good week and caught a lot of birds, we could send them to different merchants to avoid flooding the market. I probably sent the birds to two or three different firms in a good week and by doing so kept the price up. The plover were sold on commission and the cheque posted to me by return. They ended up on the tables of the smart London restaurants where customers regarded them as a great delicacy. The plover-catching season started on 1 September and ended on 1 March. Since 1947, however, plovers have been protected birds; now we are only allowed to net them under the supervision of the Royal Society of Ornithology for ringing purposes, and they must be released as soon as they have been ringed.

8
Mole-catching

When I was twenty-one I married a local Welney girl. My wife's family, like so many other Fenland families, lived off the land. My father-in-law was a fruit-grower and had also been employed by the Middle Level as a mole-catcher for twenty years. Soon after our marriage he became ill and asked me if I would take over his job until he recovered. I agreed to do it quite happily, confident that it would be easy. During my school holidays I had often accompanied one of the old mole-catchers from Welney, following him for miles along the banks and helping him to set his traps.

When I started out as a mole-catcher on my own, however, it did not take me long to realise how little I really knew. The work was quite different from what I actually imagined, and without my old friend there to help I was not very successful. Before you catch a mole you must know where it is tunnelling so that you can set your traps in the right place. Moles have runs just as we have roads and they travel up them every day, so in order to catch a lot of moles it is essential to know where these runs are. At first I used to take twenty traps out with me and just set them where I saw a lot of molehills, and I was amazed when I hardly ever caught a mole. I just could not understand what I was doing wrong. What I did not realise was that a molehill merely indicates where the moles have been digging for worms, and they are not necessarily evidence of where the main runs are. I learnt by experience but it took me a long time. Today I can take a walk along the banks and know immediately if there have been any moles about, even if there is not a molehill in sight; and I can set a trap and always be sure of catching some moles.

Last week I set some traps by the steps near my house and caught four moles, and yet there was not a molehill to be seen.

When I want to catch a mole I look for small dips in the ground which would probably not be obvious to most people, but would make me suspect that there was a mole run underneath. I next use my spud — a special spade about three inches square — and I prod about in the ground with it until I find the main run. Then, still using my spud, I dig a hole just large enough to take a trap. I put the trap down with grass on either side and a little earth on the top — not too much, otherwise it would prevent the trap from springing. The trap must fit tightly into the hole so that when the mole comes along the run it has to go through the trap and cannot pass round it. There is a tongue fixed onto the trap which is very sensitive and it activates the trap as soon as the mole touches it. Some traps will catch two moles at once, but I never use them because they are extremely sensitive and difficult to set. They keep going off and nipping your fingers if you are not careful.

My father-in-law died a year after I was married and I was persuaded by the authorities to continue mole-catching. I didn't mind because I discovered that I could combine my work as a mole-catcher with my first love, which was punt-gunning. The Middle Level paid me thirty shillings a week for the work, and I could please myself when I did it. Some days if there were a lot of ducks about I spent the day out in the washes in my punt, and I made up the time mole-catching another day.

I was not very successful at all in that first year, and although I accepted the job after my father-in-law's death I had already decided that if I did no better in the following year I would let someone else have a go. One day I was having my lunch in the pub at Purl's Bridge, about six miles from Welney, when an old mole-catcher who worked one of the other banks walked in. After greeting me, he asked, 'How are you getting on with the moles, then?' I explained to him that as I was not catching as many as I should, I was planning to give the job up the following season. 'No, you mustn't do that,' he said. 'When we've finished our lunch how would it be if I came along with you and gave you a few tips?'

I accepted his offer gladly and about half an hour later we crossed the river. As we walked along the bank he taught me all kinds of things about moles which I did not know. He pointed out the signs on the ground indicating mole-tunnels and taught me how to tell the difference between old, abandoned runs and ones which were still in use, by pressing my heel into a run, and then looking at it the following day. If the heel-print showed any sign of disturbance I would know that moles were still using that run and I should set my traps there. If there was no disturbance it would be a waste of time to set any traps. After that afternoon with the old mole-catcher I became much more competent and therefore happier in my work. I continued to do the job for another seventeen years, learning more and more about moles all the time. I relinquished the job during World War II, because at that time I was catching plovers and selling them to the London markets where they were making a lot of money. I was persuaded to take the work up again in 1947 because the Great Ouse River Board, who then owned the banks, still hadn't found anybody to replace me.

I went mole-catching from October to February. At other times of the year there were cattle on the banks, so I was unable to set my traps. I always started work at seven o'clock in the morning, after first having had a shot with my punt-gun. I went up to Welney Bridge with a mole-bag containing my traps and my spud and set out along the banks. I walked about twenty miles a day, ten miles up the bank and ten miles back. I set my traps on my outward journey, stopped to eat lunch, and then checked them on the way back, re-setting them again if necessary. Moles work three or four times a day, so when I walked up the banks I would probably find nine or ten moles in the traps I had set the previous day. On my return journey, hopefully, there would be several more. After I had removed them from the traps, I skinned them, stretched the skins on a flat board, tacked them down and left them to dry. Later I sold them to people in Wisbech for fourpence each. I often earned as much money in one week from selling skins as I did from trapping moles. I used to throw the carcasses down on the banks where they were eaten by herons or just rotted away.

I always worked on my own, but had my old labrador Rex with me for company. He loved to come, because in the old days there were always several hares on the banks and sometimes Rex had three or four courses a day. If a hare got up he would go and chase it all over the bank until exhausted. When he could run no more he returned to me, tongue hanging out and panting hard. If I tried to call him back and he took no notice I gave him a good hiding when he did return and he would just stand there, look at me and then lick my face as if to say, 'Sorry!'; but as soon as another hare appeared he would be off again like the wind.

If there were a lot of moles about I poisoned them instead of using traps. I used strychnine which was easy to get in those days. You did not need a special certificate, or have to sign forms, or anything like that to obtain it. It was a quick method and I could poison more moles in a day than I could trap in a week. In fact, if I wanted a week's shooting, I put poison down instead of traps and I probably killed more moles then than I did in two or three weeks of trapping. The disadvantage of this method was that I didn't get the skins to sell. However I probably earned an extra ten pounds shooting ducks, so it generally worked out all right financially.

The night before laying the poison I got some crochet cotton and cut it into short lengths, which I dipped in the strychnine and left to dry. The following morning I set out with my bundle of treated cotton, a big tin of worms, a darning needle with the eye cut out at the top and my spud. When I came to a run I dug a hole and using my needle pushed a piece of the poisoned cotton into a worm, put the worm into the hole and covered it up. Strangely the worm was not affected by the strychnine very quickly, perhaps not for a day or two; but as soon as the mole ate the worm it would be dead. I never attempted to remove the dead moles but always knew if the poison had worked because they would not kick up any more hills.

Obviously, I was always very careful when handling strychnine and washed my hands thoroughly after using it, but I knew a man by the name of Ike Thompson who never took any precautions. He used to come to our house to mix the poison for me and treat the cotton when I first started trapping. He would arrive at the house often carrying a large bundle of cotton which he had already treated. It was usually all stuck together and he'd pull off a bunch for me, perhaps the width of two fingers and say, 'Here you are, that will last you for a time.'

Then he would put his hand into his pocket, pull out his tobacco pouch, roll a cigarette and smoke it, without even bothering to wash his hands. It was amazing, because I never knew him to be ill. In fact he's still alive and well today at the age of eighty-five.

Moles have extremely sharp teeth and have been known to kill rats, and you have to be very careful how you pick live moles up. Sometimes when I was out with my old dog he would sniff out a mole if it was close to the surface, and he'd start scratching frantically at the earth with his feet, kicking up a cloud of soil behind him in his efforts to reach the mole. If he succeeded and managed to pick it up, the mole often bit his ears and then just hung on to them. The poor dog would yelp and then come whimpering to me and I had to squeeze the mole to get it off his ears before I could kill it. To do this you have only to tap it on the head; the blood runs out of it in a moment and it is soon dead. Moles do not take much killing.

Today there are no professional mole-catchers and that is why there are so many moles about. The River Board usually approaches one of the men in their gangs and says, 'Right, you can go mole-catching today.' They don't seem to realise that it is a skilled job. Just as a mechanic has to be trained to do his job in the proper way, so a mole-catcher has to be taught; and he will continue to learn something new nearly every day, often by his mistakes. My wife's grandfather said to me, 'The birds will teach you about shooting,' and so they do. It is just the same with the trapping business, but you must have someone to show you how to get going.

9

Baskets, Eel-traps and Grigs

My father had a basket-making business which he ran from his shop near Welney Bridge, which spanned the Old Bedford and Delph rivers. He grew his own willows by the side of the Delph and in spring and autumn hired some local men to cut them for him. The willows which were cut in autumn were unpeeled and known as brown willows; the ones which were cut in spring were peeled and referred to as white willows. They always had to be cut and peeled when the sap was rising because they were easier to peel then and a nice, white colour underneath.

After the men had cut the willows, they tied them into bundles and loaded them into a boat. A strong line stretched from the boat to the bankside and a man, walking along the bank, hauled the boat to the 'Halts'. This is a patch of land by the Delph, close to Welney Bridge, which has belonged to our family for generations and today we still refer to it as the 'rod-peeling place'. It was here that the willows were unloaded from the boat by my father and Joey Butcher and passed on to a group of women who worked for my father every year peeling the willows. They were a familiar sight in the springtime, sitting in the shade of the trees, three rows of them, all wearing large white bonnets, whistling and singing or chattering to each other all day long as they worked. They rarely stopped for a break because my father paid them according to how many bundles of willows they stripped. To do this they used a rod-peeler, which was basically a square stake hammered into the ground, with two fangs on the top controlled by a spring. The fangs operated like a pair of scissors; when the rod was placed between them they closed up and as it was pulled through, the peel was stripped off. The rods were then laid out to dry, and when they were thoroughly dry they were bundled up; some were taken to my father's shop, and the surplus was sold to other basket-makers.

My father employed two men in his shop, and together they made clothes-baskets, bread-baskets, children's cots and table-mats out of white willows, and with the brown willows they made all the baskets used by the farmers in this area and for many miles around. We used to sell thousands of them, all shapes and sizes. There were skeps in which feed was carried to the stock, the large baskets used by potato pickers and funnel-shaped ones called sack-holders. These were put into the tops of potato sacks when they were being filled so that the potatoes went straight into the sack and not all over the place.

I learnt to make baskets simply by watching the men at work and copying what they did, but basket-making never really appealed to me. My father wanted me to take over the business because in those days there was a good living to be made from it, especially as we grew our own willows, but it just did not interest me. I preferred to be outside, either on the river or in the washes. Only one aspect of the trade interested me and that was the making of eel-traps and grigs. There were three or four old eel-trappers, including my father, living in our village, and as a young boy I used to follow them around and watch them setting their traps in the river each night. The following morning I would get up early so that I could go with them again to check their traps and see how many eels they had caught. After a time I was not satisfied with just watching the eel-trappers; I wanted to have a try at catching some eels on my own, but first I had to have my own traps. I went up to my father's shop one day and he showed me how to make my first eel trap. I enjoyed doing it because I knew that when I had finished I would be able to catch some eels for myself. I made it out of willow and even today, after all those years, I am still making traps in the same way. Many people use wire because wire traps last a long time, whereas traps made out of willow only last two years and then have to be replaced. I prefer to use willow, however, because eels are fond of sucking it and so the traps themselves act as bait.

After I'd finished making that first trap I made about another thirty for myself so that I had plenty to set in the river. Inevitably word soon got around the village that I was making eel-traps and I began to get orders from other trappers. I quickly realised that I could sell all the traps I could produce, so in the winter months, when I had some spare time, I used to sit in the shed at home making them.

I have always made them out of two-year-old willows because they are fairly thick, and each willow has to be split into three and then pulled through a trimmer which cuts out the pith and makes it pliable. I cut the willows myself in October when the leaves have gone and then I can work with them right through the winter without having to soak them. If there is any willow left in March it may need soaking a little, but usually I have used it all up by the end of February.

Now I make both traps and grigs. Grigs are basically the same shape, long and cylindrical, waisted in the middle and with large cylindrical heads. The eel swims in at the head, passes through what we call the two 'chairs', but which is in fact the waist, and into the narrow end, where it is trapped because it is unable to turn around and swim out again. The differences between traps and grigs are in size and function. A trap is between three and four feet long and about two feet in circumference. A grig is three or four times as long, with a large head. Traps are baited, but grigs are not as they are used alongside eel nets which are thrown into a river to enclose a section where eels might be.

When I was using eel nets, I put them into the river and then threw in about half a dozen grigs in front of the nets. The eels swam up to the nets and, when they discovered that they could not get any further, turned around and swam into the grigs head-first. When they reached the 'chairs', they always turned round and swam in backwards, tail first and were trapped. Each grig can hold about two stones of eels and I often had them full.

When I first started eel-catching my father showed me how to bait the traps with worms threaded on to copper wire and wrapped round a spindle of wood, which was inserted into the trap through a hole near the waist. Sometimes I was up half the night with a torch after a shower of rain, collecting worms which lay on the top of the lawn. He also taught me always to set my traps under the old willow trees which overhang the river, because the leaves fall from the trees and drop into the river among the stumps, and there the eels like to settle because they are so fond of sucking the bark of the willow.

May and June are the best months for catching eels, especially if there has been a flood. I set my traps early in the evening before the sun goes down and then get up early the following morning, as soon as it is light, to check them. If it has been a mild night and the ground is covered with little blobs of earth thrown up by the worms, I could always be sure of catching plenty of eels. They are a bit like sheep; they like to follow one another. If one swims into a trap, the rest tend to follow. Sometimes I used to catch up to forty stones of eels at a time, but no one else knew how many I was catching unless they were up and about when I was taking the eels out. This was unlikely because it was often about four o'clock in the morning, when most people were still in bed. There's nothing like being up at that time in the morning for seeing birds on their nests, otters fishing and, above all, breathing in that lovely, sweet-smelling fresh air.

Occasionally when I was setting my eel-traps I put out about a dozen eel lines up the middle of the river. They are long, just like fishing lines, attached to pieces of wood about three feet long. The lines are weighted and have a hook on the end where I put small eels for bait. Sometimes I caught eels weighing five or six pounds on these lines. I remember one morning going up the river in my boat to check my lines and as I started to pull one of them in, an otter's head appeared above the water, level with my boat. It was hanging on to a live eel caught on my line. I don't know who was more surprised, me or the otter! It had obviously gone for the eel on the line, but when it saw me it released the eel and quickly disappeared under the water. I have also caught pike on my eel lines.

If it was a wet day and I could not do any other work, I would go out in my boat with my gleve, a spear-like instrument with four or five fangs fixed on to a long pole. I would keep stabbing the gleve repeatedly into the bed of the river in the hope of spearing a nest of eels. If I struck lucky, I caught the eels between the fangs of the gleve and hauled them into the boat, where I had a wooden box with a piece of wood nailed across the middle. I stuck the fangs of the gleve into the piece of wood and twisted them so that the eels dropped into the box below. On a good day I could catch about a stone of eels in an hour, and in the afternoon I went round the village and sold them to make a little extra money, because in those days if you did not work you got no money!

I have always enjoyed eel-catching and in my younger days it fitted in well with my other work too because the eel-catching season stretches from April to October and I was not mole-catching, wildfowling or plover-catching during these months. When I went out I never knew what I was going to catch or see. Occasionally I have caught lamprey eels, perhaps only one or two a year and always on the spring tide. They are tortoise-shell in colour. The old fishermen called them nine-eyed eels because they appear to have nine eyes on their backs and they have a sucker mouth underneath. Some people claim that they do not exist, but I know they do because I have caught many in my time — in fact I still do. Another eel, which is now almost extinct, was known to the old eel-trappers as the 'eel pout'; I believe the proper name is the burbeck, and I have only caught odd ones in my traps. They are half fish, half eel; not as long as ordinary eels, but fatter.

When I think about them I realise what wonderful

creatures eels are. Born in the Sargasso Sea, millions of them start the long journey to these rivers, yet only a small proportion actually arrive here. The rest of them are eaten on the way by the predators of the sea. When they first come here they are only tiny and known as elvers, and stay for several years, growing to about five or six pounds. When they are fully mature they change colour from yellow to silver and make their way back to the Sargasso Sea where they spawn and die.

I still make eel-traps and grigs each winter, sometimes for myself, often for professional eel-trappers or for people who simply enjoy catching and eating eels and who perhaps live near a culvert where they can put down a trap and catch a few. Occasionally, I make them for schools or museums as examples of a craft which unfortunately is rapidly dying out. In days gone by, not only did the old folk eat the eels, they also used to make garters from the skins because they were very tough. Some of the old women used to say that garters made from eel skins, if worn correctly, kept rheumatism away; but I don't know how much truth there is in that.

10
Fen Skaters

When I was a young lad the winters seemed much colder than they do today and whenever there was a freeze up, crowds of people from miles around flocked to Welney for some skating. Standing on Welney Bridge and looking across the frozen rivers and washes you could see hundreds of tiny figures, heads down, hands behind their backs gliding smoothly, backwards and forwards across the ice.

Skating was a very popular pastime in those days and nearly all the men and boys from our village owned a pair of skates. I was ten when I got my first pair, and they were wooden ones with turned up toes called 'Fen Runners'. Like all the other local children I taught myself to skate by pushing a chair along the ice in front of me. I loved it, and at night I used to pray for a keen frost; when my prayers seemed to be answered and there was ice on the washes, out would come my skates.

My mother was always worrying about me in case I fell through the ice. She would never allow me out with my skates until she knew that John Cam, one of Welney's oldest skaters and renowned for being careful, had been out skating. She knew that he never attempted to go onto the ice until it was thick enough to bear his weight, so if he was on it she knew that I would be safe. I remember how I used to stand on the bridge outside my house, impatiently looking out for the old boy. As soon as I spotted him on the ice I rushed in shouting to my mother, 'He's there, he's skating!' But she always had to go outside and look for herself to make sure that it really was John Cam that I'd seen, before she said to me, 'All right, off you go!'

By the time I was twelve I was quite a good skater, and

when I was about fifteen a big skating match was staged in Welney. It was classed as a Junior event and anyone below the age of sixteen was allowed to enter. Boys from all over the Fens and surrounding districts came to compete along with the local lads. Of course I entered, with all my mates, and I managed to come second. My father who was watching the match from the bankside was quite impressed and thought that I showed some promise as a speed skater, so he went out the following day and bought me a new pair of skates. They were Norwegian, similar to ones that Jim Fish, the famous local skater, had brought over from Norway in the eighteen-nineties. I was really pleased with them and whenever the opportunity arose and there was enough bearing ice on the washes and rivers I was out on my skates practising, sometimes skating as much as twenty miles a day along the frozen rivers. I was full of enthusiasum for the sport and soon started competing regularly at skating matches. It was not long before I discovered that I could beat all the old champion skaters from round here who had by then passed their prime and this gave me extra confidence.

I took my skates to Mr Prior, the village blacksmith, to have them sharpened. His shop was by the church and it was a popular meeting place for the men of the village, especially in wintertime, when they gathered there in the warmth for a gossip and to exchange a few jokes. Occasionally, a conversation which started out as a friendly discussion developed into a fierce argument. When this happened tempers grew hot and sparks flew not only from the anvil! Most of the time, however, the atmosphere in the smithy was warm, cheerful and friendly.

One day as I walked in with my skates, Mr Prior was talking to Johnnie Blows, the village carpenter, who had a shop next door to the smithy. I heard them discussing my performance on the previous day at a skating match at Outwell. When the carpenter turned and saw me standing in the doorway he said, 'I just don't know how you came to beat all those old skaters at Outwell yesterday.' Old

Prior — I can see him now — pulled out his enormous leather apron, shook it over the anvil and said, 'Well, John, you know what beats good old skaters — good young ones!' I have never forgotten those words.

After competing as an amateur for several seasons, I decided to turn professional at the same time as a friend of mine, Billy Scott, who lived in Welney. He was a very good skater and hard to beat. We started to travel all over the country to compete in matches and we soon became quite well known. Telegrams began arriving at my house from clubs in other areas, inviting Billy and I to take part in skating matches or give exhibitions. We had to cycle to Ely Station and then take a train to wherever the event was being staged. Usually when we arrived to compete in a match, we'd find that a small tent had been erected close to the course, where we could change into our racing gear just before the start of a match. I raced in a black leotard-type suit with a skull and crossbones painted on the back in white. At the end of the race, when we returned to the changing tent, there was often a glass of whisky waiting for us, thoughtfully provided by T. T. Ward, one of the farmers who lived in this area. He was one of the regular time-keepers at these events and a really kind old boy, who always took a bottle of whisky with him to matches to share with a few of the top skaters.

Sometimes Billy and I were invited to take part in three or four different matches on the same day. When this happened we tried to organise our day so that between us we would be able to cover all the matches. This meant that we often had to travel in opposite directions; Billy going to Ely and me to Crowland, for example. More often than not we both won our matches and on our return to Welney we met in the pub to share the prize money and discuss the day's skating over a glass of beer.

I did not win every race: a lot depended upon the state of the ice. I preferred to skate on soft ice because then I was fairly certain of beating my opponent. Occasionally in practice, I skated when the ice was too soft and fell through it. When this happened it was a struggle to get back on the ice again, because when the water is three or four feet deep it is very difficult to climb back on to the top of the ice with skating pattens on.

I never knew of anyone about here drowning whilst skating, although there were several accidents and people fell in. During a freeze up the ice on the washes would bear a horse in some places, but in others it would not support a small child. The wildfowl were responsible for this. During the daytime they would keep the ice around them open, but when the temperature dropped during the night those holes made by the birds during the day froze over. If there was a sprinkling of snow in addition to the frost, the great expanse of ice in the washes would appear flat and even. There would be nothing to indicate to the unsuspecting skater that there were patches of very thin ice and this led to several accidents.

One day my brother and I were skating on the washes with several friends, when one of them hit one of these patches of thin ice and fell in. At first no one offered to go to his assistance for fear that they would fall in too, but it soon became apparent that something would have to be done quickly because he was in obvious danger. My brother, Reg, took off his overcoat, carefully approached the man and, going as close as he dared, threw his coat at him. Luckily the man managed to catch hold of one end of it and my brother, holding the other end, slowly pulled him out of the water and on to the top of the ice. The rest of us stood around in silence, watching and hardly daring to breathe in case the ice cracked again, until at last he was safe on firm ice. Reg certainly saved his life that day because he had been submerged up to his neck and would soon have frozen to death. My brother Reg has been dead now for fifty years, but the man whose life he saved still remembers him. His name is Keith Malkin and his parents kept The Crown at Suspension Bridge; a pub which closed down many years ago. I often see him when I go to Ely market and he still talks about that day.

On another occasion a man was skating close to the railway bridge when suddenly the ice cracked and he fell in. Fortunately some men happened to be working on the bridge at the time and they threw a rope down to pull him out, but just at that moment a train was heard approaching. They knew that there was no chance of rescuing him before the train arrived at the bridge, so they tied the rope to one of the supports and left the poor man dangling in mid-air until the train had passed. He said afterwards that it was the longest train he had ever known!

Up until 1929 all our races had been skated along rivers. Markers were put by the sides of the rivers to indicate the course and a beer barrel was placed in the centre at each end. The barrels were half a mile apart and you had to skate so many times around the barrel, depending upon the distance of the race. Each time you skated up to a barrel a few seconds, perhaps five or six, would be lost. The rivers were long and narrow and you always had to slow down before you reached a barrel so that you could skate round it. Then it took another few seconds to gather momentum to skate down the straight stretch again.

Speed skating really changed in 1929 when the organisers of skating matches decided to start using the continental type of courses. They were circular instead of straight which meant that they were faster.

I remember clearly the first race I skated on a continental course because the event took place on the day my second daughter, Hazel, was born. I was woken by my wife during the night and I had to get up and cycle seven miles to Upwell to get Doctor Barraclough to come and attend to my wife. After the baby was born I left home to go to Swaversey, where the race for the Swaversey Cup was to be held on the new type of course. The date was 28 February, and it was a bitterly cold day; in fact it was so cold that when I arrived at the course I decided not to change into my racing kit but to skate in my ordinary clothes instead. I remember that there was an unusual air of excitement amongst both the spectators and the competi-

The man said 'It's the longest train I've ever known'

tors that day, and a great deal of speculation about how the skaters would perform on the new circular course and whether any records would be broken. Billy Scott and I were both skating and a good crowd of supporters travelled from Welney to cheer us on. Billy came first and I came second, but no records were broken as far as skating was concerned, although it still stands out in my memory as the coldest day I have ever known. At home we had to melt snow in the kettle because everywhere was frozen tight and there was no running water.

Soon afterwards the English Championships were held at Lingley Fen on the old conventional type of course. A coach-load of supporters travelled from Welney, confident that either Billy Scott or I would win the championship. To everyone's surprise we were both outskated that day by a fellow called Don Pearson who had been beaten by both Billy and I on several occasions that season. Later we learned that on the day prior to the race, Pearson's father had bought him a new pair of skates and on them he had recorded a time of exactly five minutes for the race which was over a mile and a half and had three turns in it. Billy's time was five minutes ten seconds, and mine five minutes fifteen seconds. The race was watched by one of our top local skaters, a man called Horne, who had just returned from Switzerland where he had been receiving some special coaching. After the race was over I was approached by Horne who told me that I had lost it because I'd been drawn, in my heat, to skate against an older man who did not push me hard enough, so I had not put enough effort into the race. In speed skating you always skate in pairs and if you are drawn against a fast opponent you know that you have to skate hard to beat him, and so you put in that extra effort and as a result record a faster time.

After Horne's trip to Switzerland he was almost unbeatable, and won nearly all the championships at various distances. In fact no one was able to beat him until about 1935, when the rink men started to come down from London to compete in our matches. They always beat the

Fen men because they skated all the year round and got plenty of practice.

The last match I took part in was at Welsh's Dam in 1933. Skaters came from all over the country to compete, including the fellow who had won the half-mile championship at Ruislip the year before. Although he was favourite to win the race I was fairly sure that I stood a good chance of beating him, because I had already skated against him several times that season and he had not even managed to come in the first eight. When the draw took place I found myself paired with him in the first heat. Determined to show him how confident I was, I did not even bother to change into my racing kit and skated in the clothes I had travelled in instead. Before I had even completed the first lap I was wishing that I had bothered to change, because there was a head wind and I was wearing plus-fours that day which did not help at all. The half mile I skated in that heat seemed more like ten; it was such hard work! Nevertheless I pushed on and was first over the line. After the heat an old bookie came sidling up to me and whispered in my ear, 'You're going to win today.' I wasn't so sure, because a man called Fred Smith was skating and I had heard that he was in very good form; I told the bookie so but he didn't appear to be bothered. He was still convinced that I would win and even promised to give me ten pounds from his own pocket if I was first over the line. He was obviously hoping to spur me on to greater effort, because he knew that the odds against me were quite high and he would be well into profit if I won.

The final was between me and Fred Smith. With the promise of an extra ten pounds, I decided to take no more chances and I changed into my racing kit; I put all my effort into pushing hard ahead right from the start of the race, and I won. After being presented with my prize money I went to the bookie and collected my ten-pound bonus. He paid up happily and was as pleased as I was with the result that day.

One afternoon when I was twenty-seven, and in my

prime as a speed skater, I had an accident with my gun and the hammer went into my knee. The mark it made was no bigger than a match-head, but when I reached home I was limping and my wife asked me what had happened. 'I've shot myself in the knee, but it's nothing to worry about, it's only a scratch,' I replied. Later that night I decided to walk up to The Eagle Tavern for a drink, and as I sat in the pub I could feel my knee swelling up, so I decided to go home early. Within two hours it was so swollen that I could hardly take my trousers off and it was aching badly. The following morning my brother came to help me to get up to the doctor's surgery. The doctor looked at it, gave it a prod, stuck a plaster on it and then sent me home.

During the following week my leg got a little worse each day and soon I was unable to stand on it. Finally my wife sent for the doctor and when he arrived he took one look at my knee and stuck a thermometer in my mouth. After reading it he said, 'You'll have to go into hospital straight away with that leg.' An ambulance arrived and I was taken to Addenbrook's Hospital in Cambridge on 23 October, my wedding anniversary. The surgeon operated on the same day and I did not come home again until the following March, very weak and walking on crutches.

Gradually I got stronger and was eventually able to walk without the aid of a stick and with no signs of a limp, but sadly my career as a speed skater was over. I never competed in another race although I have skated miles since that accident. In fact I can still skate today, but only for enjoyment.

11

The War Years

My contribution to the war effort between 1939 and 1945 was to join the fire service. At the beginning of the war several of the men from our village banded together and formed a fire-fighting crew, which was responsible for extinguishing any fires caused during enemy attack. In fact, although we attended several fires during the war, not one was caused by an enemy bomb!

We established our headquarters at the Cherry Tree, a pub at the end of the village. A telephone was specially installed there so that we could be summoned quickly should a fire break out. Just as in the larger fire stations we divided ourselves into two teams, six men in each, and we worked in shifts, so that there was always a team on standby at the Cherry Tree each night.

The first piece of fire-fighting equipment we were issued with was an old hand pump, which had to be operated by four or five men standing at each side of it. Later Wisbech fire station let us have one of their fire engines. Although it was an old model with solid tyres, it was still a nice little engine and a big improvement on the hand pump. As the war went on, trailer pumps were introduced and we were issued with a Beresford Stork Trailer pump.

Initially we had to go to Downham Market every Sunday morning for training in fire-fighting. We were drilled and taught to use the various kinds of fire-fighting appliances and each man in the team was given his own special job to do. For example, the first man had to go for the hose which he coupled to the engine; the second man had a hose which he coupled to the first one and so on, until the hose was long enough to reach from the engine to the fire. Next one of the men attached the nozzle on to the hose and shouted, 'Water on!' This was repeated by everyone along the line until the message reached the man at the engine who turned the water on. Two men held the nozzle and pointed it at the fire and as the water pressure from the engine increased, a third man stood behind them to support the hose. This exercise had to be repeated over and over again, until we were able to do it as speedily and efficiently as possible. Eventually we managed it in exactly two minutes from start to finish.

The first fire we were ever called out to was at Nordelph, about four-and-a-half miles by road from Welney. We were sitting in the Cherry Tree when the call came through. A trailer had caught fire and the flames had quickly spread to a nearby straw stack. We rushed out, climbed into the truck which was already attached to the trailer pump and raced out of the village along the Nordelph Road. As soon as we reached the fire we jumped out whilst the truck was still drawing to a standstill, and proceeded to put all the training we had received into practice. We soon had the fire under control and managed to prevent it from spreading to other stacks. Two more fire-engines from Downham Market and Outwell turned up later, but the work was almost done and after about two hours we were able to go home.

On another occasion we had to go to Wissington sugarbeet factory where the pulp had caught fire. Unfortunately it is not possible to put out a pulp fire, so we had to take it in turns with other teams of firemen from the area to keep an eye on the pulp which burned for about a fortnight. It was very boring just sitting there watching the smouldering pulp and time passed slowly.

One day there were six of us from Welney on duty at Wissington; there was nothing to do, so we decided to relieve the boredom a little by having a game with the hoses. We turned the water on and directed our hoses on to the corrugated iron roofs of the factory. Standing about fifteen yards away, we soon discovered that when the

The corrugated sheets rose into the air like feathers

pressure of the water was high enough we were able to lift the sheet of corrugated iron up into the air like feathers. We started competing to see who could lift the roofs the highest. After that we had contests to see who could hold them up in the air the longest. It was great fun.

One night, after we had been fooling about, we laid the hose down on the ground whilst we had a smoke. The water was still on and a young messenger lad from the local fire station, who'd called to see us, spotted the water gushing out from the hose. He could not resist the temptation to pick up the hose and spray some water around. As he was struggling to lift it up who should walk around the corner but the chief fire officer who caught the full force of the water and was knocked to the ground. Before he had a chance to pick himself up, the young lad disappeared, and we never saw him again.

Our team was returning from Wissington at daybreak one morning after being on duty at the fire all night. It was very foggy and we got completely lost, because it was impossible to tell which direction we were travelling in. To make matters worse, there were no road signs to tell us where we were because they had all been taken down at the start of the war, to prevent the enemy from finding out where they were should they happen to land. As we crawled along in the truck we met a group of farm labourers setting out for work. They were true patriots, because when we pulled up and asked them where we were, they just stared at us and refused to say anything. They were obviously very suspicious of us and probably thought that we were a bunch of German spies! We had no idea where we were that morning and we wandered for miles along tiny country roads before we eventually came to the main road where we recognised some familiar landmarks and were able to set a course for home.

Being in the fire service had many lighter moments. I remember once during a practice session we were told to wash down the village church using water drawn from the river. We set about the task very conscientiously at first, training our hoses on to the walls of the church and giving them a good wash. All was going well for a while until suddenly one of the firemen switched his hose around and directed it at one of his mates and drenched him. Although dripping with water, the other fireman was quick to retaliate and he turned the full force of his water jet onto his mate and soaked him. Soon we all joined in. The hoses were fully turned on and before long we were knocking each other over like ninepins. The church never did get properly washed down that day because we were too wet to finish the job. We all went home dripping wet and smelling far from fresh!

Welney lay directly under the flight path of the German planes as they flew over on their bombing missions, their targets being large towns and military installations in the south and midlands. Fortunately there are miles of open country around us with a relatively small population, and as there was nothing of strategic value in this area during the war we escaped any direct attacks. Occasionally a few stray bombs landed in the washes but did not do any damage. The most serious incident was when a bomb just missed Suspension Bridge, lifted the tiles of the roofs of some cottages nearby and blasted a few doors off their hinges. There were, however, several plane crashes near the village.

One day I was out in the washes when a Mustang flew over, obviously in trouble. It had petrol tanks on each wing and the pilot jettisoned them close to me as he passed overhead. One of the tanks was full of petrol and it exploded as it hit the ground. The other was empty, so I picked it up and brought it home; put it in the garden and planted flowers in it. I still have it today. On another occasion a Lancaster bomber crashed in the washes but all I could find of that were tiny fragments that had blown off on impact.

One morning one of our planes shot a Heinkel down in the washes. I hurried over to see if anyone was injured, but when I got there, there was no one around; it was obvious that the crew had escaped. In fact, the pilot had already gone to Suspension Bridge and given himself up and the rest of the crew, who had baled out, were picked up in various places in the washes later that day. Smoke was billowing out of the old plane and one of the wings was on fire so I was unable to get too close to it. Some days later I saw eight or ten trainer planes land in the washes close to the Heinkel. The airmen got out, walked round and inspected it and then flew off again. Later trucks arrived and towed the wreckage away.

Welney was about twelve miles away from the RAF base at Mildenhall. When I was out punt-gunning I often saw the bombers and fighter planes from Mildenhall out on practice flights up and down the washes. One bomber would fly over with a sock trailing behind it and the fighter planes would follow, constantly firing at the sock. One day a poor woman in Denver was killed during one of these exercises. I had one or two narrow escapes myself: for example, one morning when I was rowing my boat along the Delph I heard the fighters approaching and saw them as they flew up the wash so I quickly rowed to the side of the bank, climbed out of the boat and ran to the top of the bank and down the other side to safety. As I did so I could hear the bullets from the fighter planes plop-plop-plopping into the water where I had just been. I don't know whether or not they would have hit me that day if I hadn't moved so quickly, but I certainly got a fright.

On another occasion I was stalking some ducks when a group of fighter planes flew over. The tail-gunners in one of the planes started machine-gunning the birds as they flew off the water. I jumped up in my boat, waving my arms, to let the crew see that I was there and the plane turned and flew over me so low that I could feel the heat of its engines. I got on to dry land as quickly as I could that day.

One foggy night in the year 1941 I was woken about two o'clock in the morning by an aeroplane flying backwards and forwards overhead. Shortly afterwards I thought that I

'Don't shoot, I'm here!'

heard someone calling 'Help!', so I went downstairs in my pyjamas and stood in the doorway, listening. I could hear nothing. My wife joined me and said, 'You must have been dreaming.'

We both stood there for a little while longer but neither of us could hear anything so we went back to bed. When the postman came with the letters the next morning he said, 'We caught a Jerry last night!' When I asked him where, he just said, 'They've got him at the Home Guard Office in the village.'

Because of what I thought I'd heard during the night I decided to go up to the village to try and find out exactly what had happened. I met old Major Wray of the Home Guard up near the Bridge and said to him, 'What about this German you captured last night?' 'German!' he exclaimed, 'Who's been telling you a tale like that? It wasn't German at all, it was one of our own blokes. He has told us that he was the last one to jump out of a Wellington bomber which was on its way home from a bombing raid in Germany. Knowing that they were running out of fuel and because it was too foggy to land, the crew started to bale out when they came over the searchlight. One of the crew managed to get to the village and he's the one we've got in the office. The other two are still missing.'

Now I knew exactly where the searchlight was over the Hundred Foot Bank and I also knew in which direction the wind was blowing that night, so I assumed that the first man to jump out of the Wellington would have landed in the washes close to the Hundred Foot where there was, perhaps, only a foot or so of water. Thinking that he was close to dry land and could easily wade out of the water, he probably shot his life jacket off. Unfortunately the water gets deep very quickly the further you get into the wash and I presumed that he had obviously walked in the wrong direction, towards the Delph and drowned.

I found the second man, Sergeant Clough, the following morning, 10 February, bobbing up and down in the water right in the middle of the wash. He had kept his life jacket on but had died of exposure. The first airman, Sergeant Beals, was difficult to find. In fact his body was not discovered for thirteen weeks because our searches were hindered by floods. In spite of this I was constantly on the look out for him. On the evening of 16 April I said to my wife, 'I'm determined to find that poor airman tonight.' 'I doubt it,' she said, 'You've covered nearly every inch of those washes.'

Not in the least discouraged I went out and had not been searching above ten minutes when I spotted him. He looked just like a football; his head and feet were under the water and just the top of his back showing above, covered with his green jacket. I must have passed close to him several times without having seen him. I came home straight away, rang the police and together we got him out. Sadly, the two airmen who lost their lives were very young: Sergeant Clough was only nineteen and Sergeant Beals twenty-one.

Later some members of the Home Guard received medals for finding the bodies; I'll never know how they qualified for them because they never went out into the washes to search for the missing men. It is no use walking up and down the bank when you are looking for someone lost in the washes; you have to be out there in a boat. If the people on home guard duty the night the airmen went missing had come down for me, I could have soon put the motor on my boat and gone out to look for them. I think that I could probably have saved them, because I was obviously not dreaming that night; I did in fact hear a cry for help.

I still have the life jacket belonging to one of those boys hanging in my shed, a grim reminder of a life which perhaps could have been saved. When the water finally went off the washes, I found a ripcord handle against the Halts. I guessed that it belonged to the survivor of that crash, because it was close to the spot where he had landed. I reported my find to the authorities and the airman came back himself to collect it. During the war, evidently, airmen kept all their ripcord handles as souvenirs, to remind them of how many jumps they had made.

A camp was established at Manea towards the end of the war to house Italian prisoners. Some of them used to come to Welney each day to work on Mrs Marshall's farm which was about two miles down the Old Bedford Bank. Although the Italians were not officially allowed to mix with local people, they inevitably came into contact with some of the villagers who soon came to accept them. Actually they got on quite well with them in spite of language difficulties. During the war Joey Butcher and his wife were both well into their seventies, but age had done nothing to mellow Joey. He still liked to spend most of his time in the pub and was more often than not 'merry'. Occasionally drink had the opposite effect on him and instead of filling him with good cheer he became bad-tempered, irrational and very jealous of his poor wife. One day he staggered home from The Three Tuns, shouting as he went through the door, 'Where are you, who have you got in there with you?' As his wife stood there in the kitchen, he pointed his finger at her and accused her of going off and having an affair with one of the Italian prisoners. Poor old Rosie was speechless at first; she didn't know whether he was joking or not, but a look at his face told her that he was serious. It did not take her very long to get her voice back or her temper up and she picked up the rolling-pin which was lying on the kitchen table, waved it menacingly at Joey and shouted, 'You go to hell on a hog Joey Butcher and don't bother to come back!'

The transition from war to peace-time in Welney caused a few ripples in the smooth, slow pace of life. The departing Italian prisoners were soon replaced on the land by local men returning from active service or prisoner-of-war camps. Although food was still rationed and in short supply it was sometimes supplemented by friendly American GIs who were stationed a few miles away at Mildenhall. In return for the hospitality which many villagers extended to the American soldiers they brought gifts of sweets, chocolates and tinned foods. The Americans were here in fairly large numbers until 1947, and most people were sorry to see them go, especially the local girls who seemed to prefer them to the Welney boys — probably because they always had plenty of money to spend and a good supply of nylon stockings!

12
Snow, Ice and Floods

The worst winter in living memory was 1947, and the rivers and washes were frozen tight. When you looked across the land it was easy to imagine that you were within the Arctic Circle. Snow blocked the roads from Wisbech to Welney and the buses stopped running. To add to the misery caused by the ice and snow, gale-force winds raced across the Fens in icy gusts. People stayed indoors whenever possible, huddled over their fires trying to keep warm: but for the birds there was no protection or comfort.

As I walked about the washes that winter with my gun, I saw hundreds of birds — pigeons, coots and moorhens — lying dead on top of the ice and snow. The land was frozen up for so long that they could not get any food. One day as I walked along Scradge Bank to Will Kent's old house, I was followed by hundreds of starving coots, obviously hoping that I would be able to supply them with some food. The wildlife really suffered that winter. One of the saddest sights I ever saw were the herons; they were pitifully thin and unable to fly because their wings were frozen to their bodies and they slowly starved to death. It was impossible to help them all; the size of the problem was so great.

On 15 March there was a blizzard all over the Fens resulting in heavy falls of snow, and this was followed by a sudden rise in temperature which marked the start of the thaw. In normal circumstances the melting ice and snow would drain straight off the land into the rivers, but 1947 was not a normal winter. The ground was rock-hard and as the snow turned into water and flowed across the still frozen ground into the rivers, the volume of water was so great that the rivers just could not hold it, and it forced its way through the banks in many places and flooded the surrounding farmland. Conditions were made much worse because the pumping stations which usually helped to drain the washes were in many cases out of action. They were blocked by ice and the debris brought down by the rivers which, by now, had turned into raging torrents. At Denver Sluice, where our water joins the Ouse and flows down to King's Lynn, the water was running in full flood. At Wellmore Sluice, about four miles from Welney where our rivers drain into the Great Ouse, they were unable to open the sluice doors at first. When they did eventually manage to force them open, men had to stand at the side of the sluice breaking up the ice so that the water could flow through. I remember it crashing, smashing and splashing through those sluice doors for several days and nights until all the ice had melted. It was terrible.

The force of the gale which was blowing at the time made matters much worse. Tiles were ripped off housetops and they whirled through the air at speed. As I battled my way along the bank past The Eagle Tavern I had to keep close to the windows to avoid being hit by tiles which were bouncing all around me. The wind actually did more damage to property in Welney than the water. During the night of 16 March water started to pour over the bank near my house and into the garden. When I got up the following morning one of my boats, which had been tied up near the house, had disappeared. I found it near Welney Bridge lying on top of the ice. Another boat which I had moored in the Delph vanished altogether; it must have got smashed up by the ice because I never saw it again.

As the thaw set in, acres of ice started to move. Some of the trees in my halts stood twenty feet high but the ice just pressed them down as it moved on and passed over the top of them. Surprisingly, after the flood, most of the trees reappeared, springing up again.

One night the water was so high it was feared that the

banks would give way. The River Board decided to keep a close watch on the situation, so that if any of the rivers did look in imminent danger of bursting their banks at any point, preventive action could be taken immediately and the people round about could be warned to get ready to evacuate their homes. A group of local men volunteered to patrol the banks and they came to my house to light their lanterns. They all had paraffin lamps just like the ones they used in stables in those days. There was a howling gale blowing outside and as soon as we staggered on to the top of the bank with our lanterns, the wind blew them out and we had to go inside again to relight them. Once more we climbed to the top of the bank and again the wind extinguished them, so, losing patience, I threw mine into the hedge and carried on without it. Our heads down, we had to force our way up the bank to Welney Bridge whilst the wind rocked and buffeted us, almost knocking us off our feet. When we reached the bridge it was completely under water but I could see something sticking up in the middle. I waded through the flood towards it followed by one of my mates. We discovered that it was a swan lying on a tiny patch of dry land on top of the bridge. I gently pushed against it with my foot, but it showed no sign of life. Turning to the fellow with me I said 'it's dead,' but I was wrong. It lay there motionless because there was so much wind. At daybreak, after walking up and down the banks all night, I returned to the bridge to look for the swan but it had gone to seek shelter elsewhere.

We were fortunate in Welney, because although the water reached the top of the banks and the wash road was flooded to a height of seven feet three inches, the banks held and gradually the water started to recede. In other parts of Norfolk the situation was far more serious because flood banks gave way and water surged through the breaches in an angry torrent, the wind piling it up into waves several feet high. Acres and acres of rich farm land were under water, some of it already sown with winter wheat. Houses and farm buildings were demolished and farm machinery lay rusting under huge lakes. Hundreds of people had to evacuate their homes and leave their precious belongings behind to the mercy of the floods, only to find them beyond repair when they were at last able to return to their homes.

Once the water started to recede, it took several weeks to drain the Fens completely because much of the pumping gear normally used to get rid of flood water had been put out of action and in any case it was not adequate to deal with the problem of floods on this scale. The government stepped in to help, and giant pumps were obtained from the Admiralty, the Army, Water Boards and private firms in various parts of the country. They even appealed to the Dutch government who had a lot of experience with this kind of problem and seventeen huge pumps were brought over from Holland with engineers to operate them. Slowly the water was pumped from the land, the breaches repaired and the banks strengthened. The work was not finished when the water had gone, because so much debris had been left on the land; uprooted trees, fences and gates; haystacks which had been shredded to bits and scattered over the countryside; tons of potatoes which the previous autumn had been neatly stacked in clamps now lay rotting in fields and ditches. Everyone, from the youngest to the oldest, helped to clear the land. People around Welney trudged up and down the banks for days, hauling carts piled high with wood barely recognisable as gates and fence posts. It was all laid out to dry and then chopped up for firewood which was evenly distributed to all the cottages along Bedford Bank.

Everyone said that it would take years before the land was any good again. Planting was obviously very late, although as soon as the land was firm enough, the farmers, with an army of helpers were out in their fields ploughing and sowing, working all through the day and the night, helped during the hours of darkness by searchlights and the headlights of cars. Fortunately it was a very good summer that year and although the crops were late, they yielded excellent results in spite of everyone's fears.

The winter of 1962–3 was another particularly severe one; it was the coldest winter in the area for hundreds of years. It started freezing in December and it lasted until the first week in March; the lowest temperature here was recorded on 23 January when there were thirty two degrees of frost. I was able to walk across the river on the ice on seventy consecutive days and the children were out there skating every day or playing on their sledges. I remember one day that five horses escaped out of the washes when I was walking up the bank. They crossed the Delph and the high bank and started to race up and down the Old Bedford river on top of the ice, just outside my house. The shepherd was sent for and he managed to herd them back into the washes again. On another occasion I took a photograph of a friend of mine driving his jeep on top of the ice in the 'pits', a stretch of water down Bedford Bank which is about twenty feet deep. On 23 January I measured the ice in the middle of the Old Bedford in front of my house and it was nine inches thick, and on 7 February it was fifteen inches thick. I remember watching Arthur Carter, one of the local farmers, sprinkle salt onto his sugarbeet to thaw the top of the land to enable him to harvest the crop before the factory closed down.

The birds were dying every day on the banks and in the washes; there were no ducks to be seen anywhere. The freeze finally ended on 5 March and on 6 March miraculously, the widgeon reappeared, the first wildfowl I'd seen for months. They were obviously as pleased as we were that the big freeze was finally over.

Conclusion

Today I walked down the High Bank and stood looking across the washes to Hagan Smart's old shooting grounds and the memories came flooding back to me. Hagan and the other old punt-gunners were a breed apart, quite different from any other men I have met. Their like will never be seen again. Most people would consider their lives hard, but I know that they would not have changed places with any man. They loved the washes and their work provided them with all the excitement they wanted from life. Stalking the birds was a challenge to them. They pitted their wits against nature and experienced a real sense of achievement when their cunning and perseverance paid off and their rewards were sacks well-filled with birds.

As my eyes wandered across the washes and gazed on the land where Will Kent used to have his plover bed, I could picture him there, pulling the old net over as the plover flapped their wings and squawked as they struggled to escape from the meshes of the net. Will, like all the old wildfowlers, was very secretive about his work and would never discuss it in front of strangers who were always regarded with suspicion and distrust by the old countrymen.

Their pleasures in life were simple; they never bothered about material possessions. As long as they had clothes on their backs and food in their larders they were contented. Their most valued possessions were their guns and they cared for them almost lovingly, carrying them with them where ever they went. The one indulgence they all enjoyed was drinking and they used to gather together in the pubs most nights. They were hardened drinkers and few men could match them pint for pint and remain on their feet.

For forty-five years of my life I went out shooting in the washes in all weathers, when it was raining, snowing and blowing. I have been lost out there in the fog, shipwrecked and frozen to the bone. Sometimes I came home with a sack full of birds and at other times with nothing. I have had a full life in those washes and spent countless days and moonlight nights out there waiting for the birds to come.

I have never lived anywhere else but Welney and have never had any desire to live in any other place. The first nineteen years of my life were spent in the Ferry House and for the last forty-four years I have lived in a cottage on the Bedford Bank. I bought it just after the war and it was here that my family of two daughters and a son grew up. One of my daughters is married to a farmer and has stayed in these parts. My other daughter became a hospital sister in Alton in Hampshire and my son was a schoolteacher, before becoming an antique dealer in York.

In recent years I have embarked upon a new career and have appeared five or six times on television, as well as broadcasting a couple of times on radio. The programmes were all about some aspect of a Fenman's way of life. In 1974 Anglia Television produced a documentary film of my life which was shown not only in this country but on the continent.

Welney has changed considerably in my life time. Some of the old cottages have disappeared and been replaced by smart modern houses. We no longer have a parson living at the rectory; now he comes to visit us once a week from Christchurch, to conduct a service in the church. The Eagle Tavern where Georgie and I spent many happy hours is no longer a pub but a private house and my old mate Georgie lies in the church yard. The Crown at Suspension Bridge disappeared years ago.

When I was a lad we were free to walk about anywhere in the washes and no one questioned what we did: now all the washes are a protected area. To the north-east of Welney Bridge they are controlled by the Wildfowl Trust and to the south-west by the Royal Society for the Protection of Birds. Change is inevitable and necessary because it goes hand in hand with progress and I welcome it; but at times I enjoy indulging in nostalgia and looking back to my happy days spent close to nature.

Index